# AUCTION
# *YOUR* HOME?
# ABSOLUTELY!

an inside guide to real estate auction

## PAM McKISSICK

*CEO of America's Leading Real Estate Auction Company*

Auction Your Home? Absolutely!
an inside guide to real estate auction

Copyright © 2011 by Pamela L. McKissick

Published by McKissick Gregory Enterprises, LLC
Tulsa, Oklahoma
www.pammckissick.com

ISBN: 978-0-9849804-0-6 (Paperback)
Library of Congress Control Number: 2011946000 (Paperback)

Book design by Matt Williams
Copy layout by Anya Hoffecker


First paperback edition

PRINTED IN THE UNITED STATES OF AMERICA

# TABLE OF CONTENTS

# DEDICATION

My thanks to business partner and friend, Dean Williams, Georgetown attorney and a gifted thought leader. He's taught me to de-label the world and give it a chance. I couldn't have a finer auction business partner.

My thanks to mentor and friend Tommy Williams, former president of the National Auctioneers Association, a brilliant auctioneer and sales strategist, who, along with his wife, Trudy, taught me the psychology of auction.

My love and thanks to my partner Cheryl Gregory, the creative and spiritual force in my life, who has partnered with me in every venture for twenty-two years, including the writing of this book.

# ACKNOWLEDGEMENTS

My deep appreciation to the talented WW auctioneers, ringmen and their teams, along with the WWM staff, who have made us the company we are today.

Special thanks to editor and friend, Dr. Shelley Thrasher, who has been my editor for several years and who graciously and expertly handled the entire editorial work on this book.

And thank you to the National Auctioneers Association and all of its dedicated, hard-working auction families who trade in real estate, art, antiques, automobiles, fundraising, personal property, livestock, and heavy equipment, helping to move America forward.

# FOREWORD

Sellers often say, "Just tell me how it works," as if their decision to auction their home should be based on some mechanical process. In fact, the decision is a psychological one. Determining if real estate auction is right for you isn't merely about the details of a listing agreement or the number of open houses or the attributes of your home. To successfully auction your home, you must unwind the numbers in your head, acknowledge the desires of your heart, and open your mind to the unimaginable freedom of letting go.

# CHAPTER 1

## HAUNTED BY THE NUMBER IN YOUR HEAD

You're in real estate purgatory—that listing experience where nothing happens, unless you count the hell of surprise showings, repairs for inspections, and so many open houses that a weekend without your real estate agent feels like infidelity.

Why is your house "showing" but not selling? Because buyers don't have to compete to own it! In fact, buyers can make *you* compete... pitting you against the seller down the street who will lower his asking price, throw in the wrought-iron lawn furniture, the off-road bike in the garage, and two tickets to *Les Misérables*—the only production lasting longer than the sale of your house.

The way you value, list, and sell your real estate is frustrating, inefficient, and simply archaic. I'm asking you to consider a smarter real estate sales method that puts you in control, lets you stop worrying, and allows you to move on with your life.

*The way you value your real estate.* If you're like many people, you're pretty certain you know what your property is worth. You've had conversations with neighbors and bankers and friends in the real estate business who know the market. You've had your real estate agent bring you comps, and you even have an appraisal tucked away somewhere in a drawer.

You believe the only reason you haven't sold your property is your agent: she isn't letting enough people know about the opportunity, or she hasn't made the people who do know about it appreciate the unique features—like the Jacuzzi® in the center of the living room.

She calls you at the last minute to show your property, never lets you know where, or if, she's marketing your home, and brings you low-ball offers! Not to mention you dread spending the time and money to fix the shower pan in the master bath and the new breaker box to pass inspection.

You're thinking that you'll probably fire your real estate agent because you refuse to sell your home until you "get what it's worth." But how will you know when you've "gotten" what it's worth?

How you monetarily "value" your real estate is tied to the psychological value you place on it. Outside of love and good health, your home is central to your wellbeing. It's the safe haven where you escape the pressures of the outside world, it's the reflection of your hard work, it's the embodiment of your lifestyle, and, equally important, it's the psychological barometer of your personal success or failure. Real estate is in your ancestral DNA.

On April 22, 1889, in the dash for land, we lined the Oklahoma borders at high noon ready to walk, run, or ride across some of the finest "unassigned land" to stake our claim, fence off the perimeter, and defend our parcels. One month later, William Willard Howard reported in *Harper's Weekly* 33rd edition that at high noon, the population of Guthrie, Oklahoma was nonexistent. By dark, the population exceeded ten thousand. "In that time, streets had been laid out, town lots staked off, and steps taken toward the formation of a municipal government. Never before in the history of the West has so large a number of people been concentrated in one place in so short a time."

Today, your defense of the land begins with your own backyard, where many a neighborhood brawl has erupted over fence lines. According to MSN Real Estate, in a single year six hundred thousand neighborhood feuds were mediated by five hundred neighborhood mediation centers across the US that specialize in backyard battles.

Google reports 255,000 books and articles on the topic of neighbor property-dispute resolution. We Americans take our property—the ground below and the air above it—very seriously.

Your home represents your dreams, your life savings, or your investment for a rainy day. Your familial nest was once your nest egg. Like many a homeowner, you believed the value of your home would always go up.

Your real estate may be a memory marker in an important relationship: the lake cottage your parents owned, the apartment building you lived in when you were first married, the ranch that started a new life in the country, the little bungalow where you fell in love, the office building where your business took root, the big rambling oceanfront where three generations have grown up.

And if nostalgia isn't enough to bind you to your real estate, there's social status. Your real estate holdings communicate your standing in the community. When you were a child, you were told to grow up strong, get a good education, find the right mate, settle down, and buy a nice little house. No one ever said buy a used trailer or a run-down rental.

If you got a better job, you got a better house. As you became more successful, you bought a weekend place at the lake or in the desert. Spurred on by your CPA's promise of tax deductions, you invested in a duplex or apartment building.

So if, one day, something happens to your marriage, your job, your goals, or your health, and you have to sell the house or you "lose" the investment property, what does that say about you? For most of us, it says we failed. And in fact that's usually some of the buzz around the neighborhood: "They over-extended themselves, then he lost his job…"

Your real estate is your psychological Samsonite. How you buy and sell it says something about you. Therefore, parting with real estate is no small matter. Getting "what it's worth" has become synonymous with getting what *you* are worth due to your efforts, intelligence, or status.

"What it's worth" has been the starter dough for entire industries and occupations: your mortgage lender who's making the loan, your real estate agent because she's been selling real estate in your neighborhood for years, and a reputable appraiser because he's trained to evaluate properties like yours and the bank wants his opinion.

Once you've spent the time, energy, and money to gather these expert opinions, you accept them as unbiased and fact-based. You "take them to the bank" literally and figuratively. But if these official guesstimates are too low to support the mortgage loan, the deal's over and no one gets paid: the real estate agent doesn't get her commission, the banker loses the loan opportunity, the EMP (electrical, mechanical, and plumbing) inspector doesn't get his fee, nor does the termite inspector, the insurance company, the attorney, the county clerk, not to mention the folks lined up to fix the roof, lay the new carpet, and become your lawn service. Let's face it; at one time or another, like fans at a pole-vault competition, we've all rooted for the appraiser: Higher, higher, higher!

Valuing real estate is a system you've lived with for so long that you don't question it. Of course, you have to know what real estate is worth! How else are you going to know what to ask for it? How else can you avoid leaving money on the table? How else can you avoid being "taken"?

The valuation number lets you sleep nights. "I'll sell my house one day and get four times what I paid for it and then move where things are cheaper." Or "If I ever get in trouble, I'll take a second mortgage on the house; I've got so much equity in it." Or "Real estate has dropped but my neighborhood holds its value."

And when that little voice in the back of your mind warns that your valuation number, your mental number, isn't necessarily the real number until you can find a buyer who'll agree with you by writing you a check for that amount, you comfort yourself with a cappuccino and another appraisal.

Your lending institution will tell you an appraisal is required. That's for their benefit, not yours. They need an appraisal to enable them to sell your mortgage. Ever gotten a mortgage with company A and then ninety days later received a letter saying you will now be making your monthly payments to company B? That's usually because your loan was sold in the secondary mortgage market, and, to complete the sale, the secondary market required an appraisal.

Ironically, if you pay cash for your home, no bank and therefore no appraisal is necessary because no loan will be originated or sold. If an appraiser were summoned immediately after you bought the home, the appraised value would most likely be the price you just paid for it, because the check was tangible proof that's what the home is worth.

So all these "values" are simply numbers in your head put there by experts who have no intention of backing them up with cash.

Our company handled the sale of a nice horse ranch with a large estate home and row after row of horse barns. Weeks before, I had phoned the local banker to ask what he was intending to loan on the home and acreage. The banker said his appraisal team was looking into the value and he would call me. The morning of the auction, he sidled up to me and sheepishly apologized for not getting back to me. "We talked about it but we're having trouble deciding what the property's worth."

"It's a little late for deciding what it's worth if you're planning on loaning the buyer the money today, don't you think?" I said.

"As soon as the auction's over, we'll loan eighty percent of whatever it brings."

The banker knew that after all the internal conversation, calculation, and price anticipation, the *bankable number* would be the one delivered at auction.

*Now let's take a look at the way you've always listed your real estate.* According to the NAR's 2010 *Digest of Real Estate License Laws & Current Issues*, there were 1,744,077 licensed real estate professionals in the US (almost 300,000 less than the year before) and 878,882 real estate brokers, roughly 150,000 fewer than the prior year. Nonetheless, real estate agents are everywhere. Finding a good real estate auction company, obtaining references, and understanding the process take a lot more digging.

Most people list and wait, hoping their homes will sell in 90 days, when in fact, according to Collateral Analytics™, a company that provides financial institutions with real estate data, the average time on market in April of 2011 was 225 days. Your agent may not want to discuss the industry's average days on market (DOM), and frankly you, the hopeful seller, may not want to hear it, simply because it's just one more worrisome piece of a stressful process.

So why don't we find a better, less stressful way? Because we are creatures of habit and tend to take what we perceive as the easiest route. We all know how the traditional real estate sales method works, and we also know some terrific real estate agents: they're our neighbor, cousin, sister, mother, and they're everywhere.

Auction, on the other hand, is not well known, seems scary and uncertain, and that's the fault of the auction industry for failing to educate people. Auctioneers are so busy selling they don't even stop to conduct an industry census. Even NAA (National Auctioneers Association) isn't certain how many auctioneers live and work in the US because the rules for licensing and record keeping are complex and vary by state. (Ironically, in 1901 we knew exactly how many auctioneers there were by state: California had 127, New York 480, Pennsylvania 313, and Texas only 27. In total, 6,924 US auctioneers, as cited in Robert Doyle's article entitled "Auctions in America 100 years Ago.")

Today, while there are thousands of auction companies, it's unlikely more than fifty specialize in real estate and routinely sell hundreds of properties at auction every month. That's why very few people know a successful real estate auctioneer. Therefore, the idea of entrusting your home sale to an auction company feels like bungee jumping off the side of the Grand Canyon.

You believe you're more in control with a real estate agent—beginning with the listing price, which, admit it, you influenced. While you believed the list price protected you by placing the appropriate value on your home, it really did nothing more than establish a goal for the real estate agent—the number you will forever blame her for not getting.

*Finally, let's look at the way you sell your real estate.* Is there anything less transparent than a brokered real estate transaction? A blind bat in a deep cave has a better chance of figuring out what's going on than a buyer and seller represented by two real estate agents. What are they saying to each other? Why does the buyer's agent talk to your agent and then your agent talks to you? You counter the buyer's offer by telling your agent how much less you're willing to accept. Your agent tells the buyer's agent who tells the buyer. In grade school, that game was called Grapevine, which, according to Wikipedia™, by definition, "The game has no winners."

Don't blame real estate agents. They inherited this system. But in today's do-it-yourself, instant-information, Google®-and-get-it world, who could ever say it's the most efficient, transparent way to sell real estate?

To recap: With the traditional method of selling real estate, you value properties using a host of experts who don't have to back up their valuation with cash. You fire and hire several agents and berate them for not getting the list price you helped them set. You negotiate offers in secret—buyer-to-agent-A-to-agent-B-to-seller, who counters agent B-to-agent-A-to-buyer. If you weren't so familiar with this bizarre system, you would run from it!

We travel to the moon, Facebook® with the world, grow organ

replacements in petri dishes. Is this really the best we can do when it comes to selling our real estate? There is a better way.

# CHAPTER 2

## MYTH 1:

### "ONLY PEOPLE IN FINANCIAL TROUBLE SELL AT AUCTION"

Society won't allow you to separate from your land holdings. Go to any cocktail party and right after you hear someone's profession, you often receive a recital of their real estate portfolio: "You probably know Fred is an attorney, and he and Emma have a home in the Hamptons."

Or "Bob's a builder and he just invested in Briar Ridge." Or "Mary works for a large insurance firm and her company just moved into the Lincoln Town Building."

No one wants to be introduced as, "This is Dwayne. He just lost his hat-n-ass-n-all the fixtures in a really big condo deal."

Real estate is prestige and power—the fulfillment of your ambitions and dreams. So if your home or business is taken away from you, then somehow your dream is unfulfilled, or at least tarnished. And if that home is in foreclosure, then somehow you failed in plain view of your neighbors. You lose sight of the fact that financial trouble is merely a moment in time.

Many business titans will tell you they were bankrupt at some point in their lives. Financial trouble was a dot on life's road, not a final destination.

According to cnn.com and bankruptcylawnetwork.com, a lot of very wealthy and well-known people have been in financial trouble personally or corporately at one time or another: Abraham Lincoln, Henry Ford, Donald Trump, Burt Reynolds, Francis Ford Coppola, Willie Nelson, and Larry King, to name only a few. Samuel Langhorne Clemens, aka Mark Twain, went bankrupt in 1894 investing in, among other things, a better steam engine. He paid off his debts in full four years later.

Today you're a seller, tomorrow you're a buyer. Today, you're in financial trouble, tomorrow you're not. Today you want to move to the lake, tomorrow you want to move on with your life. Life circumstances dictate the need for real estate liquidity, and foreclosure is one of those circumstances, but not the only one. Auction doesn't signal financial trouble any more than the two-minute drill in football signals a loss. Auction comes to the forefront when it's time to get serious and pick up the pace.

Farmers and ranchers love auctions. They trade cattle, equipment, and everything else at auction, so obviously when it comes time to sell their beloved homestead, they do it in the same fashion. They're not in financial trouble, they're experiencing a life transition. Their kids live in the city and don't want to run a large ranch, or they've sold pieces of their land over the years and don't have enough to make farming profitable. They're too old to work outdoors the way they used to. It's not foreclosure but it is closure, and equally hard on them. They don't want to watch strangers parade through and lament that the kitchen isn't updated and the bath is tiny or how they're going to tear up a pasture and build a go-kart track. They want the sale to happen reliably and quickly, the same way they moved their herd.

Trust attorneys utilize auction because of their fiduciary responsibility to stakeholders and the judiciary, and the need to prove that they're selling an asset appropriately and for the most money possible.

Wealth managers understand the need to make real estate as liquid as shares of IBM, and in fact we have clients who are third-generation sellers. They're comfortable with, and prefer, business arrangements that are fast, effective, and yield current market value.

Bankers suddenly find themselves in the real estate business and don't want to be. They often choose to sell the land assets on their books to improve their bank ratios.

Thousands of individual sellers now believe auction is the best way to quickly sell and re-invest. These people aren't in financial trouble.

They're looking out on the horizon and taking immediate steps to keep their future strong.

Nonetheless, to understand some of the fear surrounding real estate auction, consider that our company utilizes the most sophisticated auction methodology in the country. We sell thousands of properties every year, traveling to the real estate and selling on the lawn. We have thirty auction teams; skilled event marketers; auctionnetwork.com where live, interactive, real-time bidders from around the globe compete with bidders on the lawn; analytic models that predict what a portfolio of residential assets will bring within plus or minus one percent; and a proprietary auction index that tracks the housing market 60-90 days ahead of the S&P Case Shiller Home Price Index™. None of that assuages sellers' basic auction angst: What will their friends think if they sell their home at auction? Will hordes of unqualified buyers be allowed to show up and watch? How can they keep unqualified buyers from even having a *look* at their estate? Surely there won't be any signs in the yard! And of course the big one: they don't want people to think they're in financial trouble.

We recently sold the fourteen-thousand-square-foot home of a wealthy individual indicted in a ponzi scheme. The US Marshall service had seized the home and we were asked to manage, market, and auction this pristine estate. The home featured elegant grounds, a media theater, an indoor basketball court, and lovely exterior tennis courts. The home was not in trouble, its owners were. At auction, the home brought far more than the reserve price (the high bid price above which the seller must sell, and below which he is not required to do so.)

Contrast that with the family estate of an oil baron who, prior to his death, was an avid world traveler and a filmmaker. His daughter contacted us about conducting an auction of their family compound in the Midwest, which included a sprawling main house that provided commanding views of the water from every room. Behind that house stood another large two-story lake home built for the children and grandchildren. A third two-story dwelling was rented to friends, and, adjacent to it, a vacant lakefront lot. The personal property included classic sports cars, African and South American artifacts. The family wanted to sell their estate and, in doing so, celebrate their father's life and work.

The auction took place on a sunny spring day on the lakeshore lawn that rolled down to the sparkling expanse of water in front of the home. Hundreds of guests and registered bidders, in summer attire, with kids in tow, sat on lawn chairs or balconies facing our auctioneers and ring men dressed in dark suits and ties. The contents of the home lined the interior rooms of the main house: artwork, gardening memorabilia, shop tools, and motorbikes spilled over onto the tree-lined drive.

The auctioneer explained who the seller was and what his life had meant to so many and that today was not only an opportunity to own a piece of the beauty he had built but to honor this family.

He explained that we'd be using our Buyer's Choice method, which means everyone is competing for "the right to choose first." If you were the high bidder you got your choice of the real estate: you could take one parcel at your high-bid amount, or two parcels for two times the high-bid amount, or all four parcels for four times the money. If you were not the high bidder and therefore lost the right to "choose first," someone might select the parcel you came to buy.

With that, the bidding began for the real estate, racing from a nominal opening bid of one hundred thousand to one million dollars. The battle was intense between a bidder on the lawn whose wife encouraged him to keep bidding and a gentleman on Auction Network®, who later said his wife was telling him to stop.

The Auction Network® bidder, who was familiar with the property but chose to bid from home a state away, won the high bid, despite his wife's concerns about his paying too much. He took parcel one—the main house. The bidding began again and the same remote bidder prevailed, taking parcel four. Again, and the same bidder took parcel three. The bidding began again, the Auction Network® bidder lost, and parcel two went to a couple on the lawn. There was applause all round as, in a matter of fifteen minutes, all four parcels (three homes and the lakefront lot) had been sold for over two million dollars and well over the seller's reserve. All the personal property was auctioned off for hours after that. Buyers interviewed on camera said they had a fabulous day at the sale. The sellers were ecstatic and the crowd clearly knew this was a celebration, not a distress sale.

In a single month our auction roster included a ranch near the home of a former President of the United States, the family home and recording studio of a globally renowned boy band, a granite magnate's 22,000-square-foot Man Cave, the former home of a *New York Times'* best-seller-list romance novelist, and one of the finest hunter-jumper equestrian centers in the US, including the high-dollar horses stabled in the US and Europe. These sellers weren't in financial trouble. They chose auction as a smart, efficient sales strategy.

# CHAPTER 3

## MYTH 2:

### "AUCTION WON'T GET WHAT MY PROPERTY IS WORTH"

Real estate is worth what someone will pay for it, not what you hope someone will pay. If the appraiser presents you with a high number, you might be ecstatic, low and you could be depressed, forgetting that neither number has any basis in reality because the appraiser is not willing to write you a check for that amount. Somewhere in your head you know that, yet you go to great lengths to try to improve the resale value of your home before listing it.

You select new vinyl siding, replant cactus around the hot tub, and paint the master bedroom Ralph Lauren Bali turquoise, ignoring the fact that equal to the difficulty of finding someone to buy your home for what you "know it's worth" is finding someone who appreciates your taste in décor and your landscaping choices and wants to pay extra for them.

In fact the two are obviously connected. Part of the monetary value you place on your home is related to the enormous time and effort you spent repairing, decorating, landscaping, and living in it.

That makes it even harder to hear a prospective buyer cruise through your open house and whisper to his wife that they can easily knock out your new walnut cabinets and remove the wall to expand the kitchen, rip out the maple chopping-block countertop and replace it with granite, and bulldoze the Japanese elm and the bonsai trees in the backyard to make room for an Olympic-size pool.

Traditional brokerage often encourages sellers to make upgrades and repairs because the house will "show better." No question that it will show better, but will it sell better? After the non-buyers parade through, oohing and aahing over the upgrades, did the guy with the checkbook pay more because of them? In effect, with all the afore-mentioned efforts, the agent and the seller are trying to change "what the property is worth" using their own standard of additive value. Meaning "of course buyers will pay more for walnut cabinets" and "exotic shrubs always improve curb appeal." Kind of like the agent who tells you to bake an apple pie during the open house because the smell reminds buyers of their childhood. I was talked into doing that and ended up with two apple pies, three unwanted pounds, no buyers, and some really weird childhood flashbacks.

You know from your own experience that additive value is

completely subjective. Your real estate sells, or doesn't, based on what it has to offer that particular buyer on that given day. The value associated with that location, square footage, and property condition is based on the subjective likes or dislikes of the beholder. That's why real estate agents often spend so much energy trying to convince the buyer that having a sunroom versus a third bedroom is actually a good thing. Or that it's easy to turn the garage into an office. If the home isn't "speaking" to the buyer, the real estate agent has to.

Buyers are amazingly inventive, their creativity limitless, their plans unique, and their competitive spirits a joy to watch. And they're smart. They know what they like, what they'll pay, and what they'll change once they own it.

If you're aware of something completely utilitarian that would enable the buyer to better assess the property—wiring repair to allow you to see the pool after dark or removal of vines that obscure a window view—then fix that. If there's structural damage, obviously, you have to disclose what you know about the house and allow the buyer and the buyer's experts to show up and decide what they think.

If you feel compelled to make cosmetic repairs because the neighbors might come to one of the open houses, or hang the flamingo wallpaper in the bathroom because you can't bear to throw it away, do it only if it makes you feel better.

Otherwise, don't get in the way of the buyers' imagination—what

23

they would do with the home, how they would change it, what a great buy they'll get because the place "needs a little work." Then bring all those people with their dreams to that home and let them compete to own it. Auction forces them to step up and do business. The couple who's had a real estate agent bring them to your home so often they're on a first-name basis with your dog has to finally quit talking, measuring, and fretting, and play and pay on a given day.

Auction basically asks buyers to acknowledge that they're adults and they can take care of themselves. If your buyer thinks the roof is in poor shape, he didn't have to demand you repair it and then, after closing on the home, complain to all his friends that you repaired it cheaply because you knew you were getting rid of it. He can acknowledge the roof isn't brand new and determine accordingly how much he's willing to bid for a home that requires roof repair.

Real estate auction will "get what it's worth." Now you have to be comfortable that it's worth what it gets.

A lovely home situated next to a nuclear power plant is in a fabulous location and worth every penny if you've landed a job there and are dying to be close to your work. A home downwind from a neighboring hog farm is a real buy if you lost your olfactory sensitivity at an early age. On any given day, "what it's worth" is a buyer decision. Sellers can suggest, demand, market, bargain, and withhold, but the buyer decides.

Put yourself in the buyer's shoes. You've decided to take your cash out of the stock market and invest in a small piece of commercial real estate.

You hear about a hotel in a nearby town of forty thousand people. The hotel cost a million dollars to build and several years ago sold for five hundred thousand. The townspeople disliked the owner and refused to step foot in the hotel, much less dine there. Ultimately it was leased for parties, proms, weddings, and conventions, and each group seemed to damage it more than the last. The hotel owner now wants to sell the hotel at auction. It's been on the market for two years and he's turned down two offers above three hundred thousand dollars.

Is this hotel the opportunity you've been looking for? You might say of course! The town would welcome new owners and be very supportive. Or you might say absolutely not—too many repairs, and the community is too small and isolated to support a hotel.

The seller decides to auction the hotel but reserve the right to reject the high bid, if it doesn't meet his expectations. Would you spend weeks doing your homework about the building, get your money together, and show up at the auction? Probably not.

If the hotel is scheduled to sell at auction without reserve (meaning the property will be sold to the highest bidder regardless of price), it's far more likely you'll show up and compete because the seller's method of auctioning signals that this time he's serious about selling.

Once you attend the auction, how much will you bid? If someone gave you a check for five hundred thousand dollars and said you could spend it on any hotel in the world, would you select the hotel I just described? If I said you had to buy this hotel with part of your five hundred thousand dollar gift and then you could buy any other piece of real estate with the remainder, how much would you allocate to the hotel?

Buyers have choices and cash buyers have infinite choices. Auction brings them off the sidelines, and the property and the opportunity sell them.

Now put yourself in the seller's shoes. You own this hotel. You know you're not an idiot so clearly the situation around this failing hotel can't be your fault. It was simply the perfect storm: bad luck due to unforeseen circumstances, the wrong community, poor timing, and not enough money to tell people about it. The new buyer, in your estimation, can easily make this hotel profitable with "just a few minor repairs and the right marketing." You might say five hundred thousand is the bare minimum that the buyer should pay for a hotel that cost a million dollars to build and could never be rebuilt for that sum.

Auction bridges the gap between buyers' desires and sellers' expectations. Auction is where real estate meets reality.

If a professional auction company effectively target-markets the property, local buyers show up on the lawn, out-of-state buyers log in remotely via interactive technology, a top-notch auctioneer handles the sale, and the registered bidders bid vigorously and then all stop at a given number, that number is current market value. How can it not be? The value of that asset on that day at that moment in time has been established, just as NASDAQ™ and the NYSE™ arrive at a value for every publicly traded stock at day's end. In both cases, the value is backed up with real money, delivered in real time.

Real estate values plummeted in 2008 and continue their downward trend. If you're lucky enough to still have a home, you may bemoan the "financial loss"…even if you never intend to sell. You've lost money because neighbors, the media, buyers of real estate, the federal government, appraisers, and bankers no longer support the value you "had in mind." The unrealized number in your head is becoming a smaller unrealized number in your head, which means, you moan, that you'll never be able to sell the property for "what it's worth." That's like saying, I had a losing season at fantasy football and now I'll never be asked to coach in the NFL®. It was *fantasy* football!

# CHAPTER 4

## MYTH 3:
### "AUCTION RUINS NEIGHBORHOOD HOME VALUES"

We humans are a fairly practical lot. If auctioning a house actually ruined the value of the homes around it, irate neighbors would have stamped out auction centuries ago, yet auction has survived for thousands of years. The reason lies in the Latin root for the word auction, *auctio*, meaning "to increase." And increase it has.

The auction industry was a $268 billion dollar industry in 2008, the last time anyone was counting. According to the National Auctioneers Association (NAA) the real estate sector grew by 47 percent from 2003-2008 as the most likely asset to be auctioned, second to auto auctions.

People often think they're embarking on something new when they go to auction, but they're actually engaging in an efficient method of trading that took place thousands of years ago, long before the birth of Christ. Clearly, auction is an old-world art with a new electronic twist, but the core principles of competition, time-definite sales, and public opportunity have worked for centuries.

Auctioneer Robert Doyle, 50th President of the NAA, is one of the foremost auction historians in the business, and my knowledge of auction history derives in part from his extensive work, which can be found in articles located on the National Auctioneers Foundation Web site.

One of the earliest recorded auctions took place in Greece in 500 BC with the annual auctioning of brides. Something as lovely and coveted as virgins required that competition prevail. In fact, it was illegal to sell a daughter outside of auction. Fathers of the less attractive daughters had to add dowries or other money to the bridal package to increase the sale price. In the "not much ever changes" category, while women had to be gorgeous and virgins, men only had to drive by with drachmas.

According to an article written in 1909 in *International Auctioneer* magazine, Frederic J. Haskin noted that the first auction, according to Josephus, first-century historian and author, occurred when the children of Israel captured a city and sold the plunder at public outcry.

Some believe an auction was noted in the Old Testament in the book of Genesis where Abraham bought the Cave of Machpelah for four hundred shekels of silver, along with the land and trees around it, as the burial place for his wife Sarah.

In Rome around the time of Christ, auctions were used to sell family estates. Marcus Aurelius sold his family furnishings and heirlooms in an auction that lasted two months, in order to raise money to pay his war debt. He preferred auctioning his belongings to taxing the people, a note obviously missed by our present-day politicians.

Roman soldiers sold the spoils of war at auction. The auctioneer was known as the "Magister Auctionarium." He drove a spear into the ground to start the auction. The auctioneer's gavel didn't arrive on the scene until centuries later.

Fifteenth-century auctions were apparently so prevalent that King Henry VII instituted auction laws that prohibited anyone from selling at public auction unless they held the office of out roper or common cryer, thus creating "licensed" auctioneers.

In seventeenth-century Europe, rather than call the crowd to the auction, they took the auction to the crowd, holding the sale where people were already gathered in coffeehouses and taverns. Personal property like art and furnishings were sold amid uplifted spirits of both varieties.

American auctions date back to the Pilgrims and the colonization of our Eastern seaboard. Trading took place between the Indians who

31

had the fur pelts and the settlers who wanted them. The settlers took the furs to the shoreline and auctioned them to merchants who transported the furs back to Europe, where another auction took place, this time among manufacturers who competed for the opportunity to process the furs and sell them to the wealthy.

In 1739 the *London Evening Post* announced a real estate auction.

Auctions worked so well that not only merchants but stockbrokers suspected auction was cutting into their income. In May of 1792, twenty-four merchants and stockbrokers in New York City convened under a Buttonwood tree to sign the Buttonwood Agreement, effectively ending all street-corner stock trading by auctioneers. Brokers could deal only with other brokers and for a specified commission. This was a public attack on auctioneers…not to mention a bit of price fixing.

By 1828 a petition was brought before Congress, signed by a number of New York merchants who wanted a heavy tax imposed on auctioneers to curtail their trading in imported goods, which the signers said ruined the market. Auctioneers fought back and won.

Auctions were common practice during the Civil War era of the 1860s. Soldiers often quarreled over the spoils of war so the commanding officer, usually the colonel, would collect the items and, to insure fairness, conduct an open-outcry auction. Modern-day auctioneers are occasionally referred to as "Colonel."

By the turn of the century, auctions were taking place for every conceivable item all over the world. A canal in England thirty-seven miles long, with twenty-nine locks and an annual revenue stream of $25,000, was sold at auction in 1908.

By 1922 a stockbroker could have his order executed by routing it to the trading floor of the New York Stock Exchange™, where it was completed via live auction. (Today that auction transaction is executed electronically.)

Technology entered the auction business in the 1990s, bringing us eBay® and along with it confidence that cyberspace purchases would indeed show up at our doorstep.

By the year 2000, most auctioneers were specializing in a particular kind of auction: autos, real estate, and cattle.

In 2007, Auction Network® launched, taking real-time, live interactive-bidding to a new level, and conducting auctions simultaneously through television, Internet, telephone, and live on the lawn.

The US Treasury Department routinely auctions all manner of securities each month.

Charity auctions are held in Beverly Hills, art auctions in New York, classic-car auctions in Arizona, thoroughbred-horse auctions in Kentucky, and auctions are held each morning around the world to sell tulips in Holland, fish in Australia, rare books in London.

If it's priceless (the "Mona Lisa"), perishable (tulips), or must be

33

equitable (one would hope that means everything that's ever sold), then it must go to auction.

Real estate is priceless. No one is making any more of it. Homes and businesses are perishable if left vacant and unattended. And certainly, real estate transactions should be equitable. In short, real estate was meant to change hands via auction.

Go to any neighborhood with a dozen homes for sale in a half-mile radius and schedule an auction. Once the auction signs go up, not one home in that neighborhood will sell until the auction takes place. After the auction, the listed homes will begin to sell immediately, because the auction has established current market value and all the other sellers will follow.

Go to any neighborhood where virtually no homes are for sale and conduct an auction. The auction will be a huge success because inventory is in short supply and many buyers will compete to own.

Auction doesn't ruin neighborhood values, it re-aligns them with the marketplace, and once that happens, homes sell, neighborhoods revitalize, and people move on with their lives.

# CHAPTER 5

## SEVEN REASONS WHY AUCTION WORKS

In his famous WW II final pep talk to the troops, George Patton said, "America loves a winner!" In fact, all humanity is obsessed with winning.

We humans created the Olympic games so entire countries could compete against one another. And when four years was just too long to wait for the next broad jump, we created the winter games so we could watch people careen down ice trails at a hundred miles an hour feet first.

NFL® football players, marathon runners, tennis champions, and boxing legends all compete as we cheer them on. And when the games are over, we tune into reality-show competitions for the best voice, best dancer, biggest weight loss, and simply who can survive.

We don't want to do anything alone; we want to compete for it or watch someone else compete for it.

An article in *Success Science* referenced a study of human brain function during the act of winning. The research took place on November 4, 2008, on the night of the presidential election. (If you're out of the scientific loop, testosterone levels, measured in saliva-decrease, usually drop in the evening hours...although many a tired working woman might find that hard to believe.) On that night, neuroscientists at Duke and University of Michigan gave voters gum to chew and collected the gum as the polls closed. More gum was distributed and later collected as Obama was announced the winner. This night the pro-McCain gum chewers' testosterone fell off the cliff while the Obama gum chewers' testosterone soared. The same thing happened to men who were tested watching sports: testosterone levels rose in the men whose team was winning. We all live vicariously, and we love winners because they are us.

Auctions are competitive, efficient, exciting, entertaining, time definite, public, and proven.

The heart of auction is competition—that moment when a buyer's heart races, and nerves he didn't know he had surface. The auction has begun and he has only moments to give up or get in. When people are competing, they do things they never thought they could, with a sense of dedication, preparation, and determination.

Competition brings out the best in people as they give their all for all kinds of reasons. And there is nothing more competitive than real estate auction because it concerns not just a ribbon, or trophy, or bragging rights...but their home.

Auction is efficient. Every time I've sold through traditional means, I've had an endless list of repairs either required or requested before I could show the house. Days stretched into months—the termite company couldn't work me in for six weeks, and the plumber showed up but didn't have the part so he had to come back next week. The lawn guy wasn't sure the spot in the middle of the yard was fungus but he would come back and do a test. "It's not fungus!" I shouted. "The faucet probably needs a new washer and we've already checked for termites." Everyone nodded agreement, but the repair people still had to show up and I still had to meet, supervise, and pay them.

Selling your house at auction requires that you disclose, not fix. What if you replant the entire front lawn in fescue and the new buyer's favorite dog is allergic to that particular grass? You'd be better off stating that buyers should note that part of the grass needs attention. If you're fretting over the pot of pansies wilting in the backyard or the dark spot on the rug in the third bedroom, relax. The new buyer isn't making his decision based on a spot or a pot. He's deciding if the location, the bone structure, the overall layout of the home speaks to him. And the louder it speaks, the higher he bids. Let the house do the talking.

Auction is exciting. It moves rapidly, and big assets and big money change hands. It combines the elements of live theater and big business. Bidders are standing in front of the home and others are logged in to Auction Network® or have dialed in via cell phone. The auctioneer covers the rules of the sale, then begins the chant that signals lives will change in the next few minutes. Everyone is stunned at how quickly your home sold, and the buyer is overjoyed that in seconds he is the high bidder and now the new owner.

Auction is entertaining. Ninety-seven percent of the people who attend auctions claim it's for the entertainment as well as the purchase. Why in the world would someone happily bid more than they intended? Because they're engaged, competing, and at the same time, entertained. Auctions draw people in and make them part of the event. What's more thrilling than having the auctioneer chant to them, encourage them, and then congratulate them for an amazing buy as the crowd applauds? They've accomplished the modern-day version of storming across the border to stake their claim. They're the winner and the home belongs to them.

Auction is time definite. You know exactly what day your house will sell. It's that tension associated with a time-definite sale that brings the buyer out of hiding and into the spotlight. There's no more, "I'll talk to my husband about it. We have a couple of other houses to look at." "The price seems a little high, we'll have to think about it." In thirty minutes this home will change hands, and the only decision the potential high bidder has to make is whether those hands will be his.

Auction is open and public. Buyers see the person next to them bidding and they hear how high that person's willing to go. If someone's bidding on Auction Network® the on-site bidder can walk over to a laptop and see the remote bidder's user name and watch the bid buttons as he bids, or stops bidding, in sync with the crowd. This gives bidders confidence that if the fellow next to them is willing to bid two hundred and fifty thousand dollars, they're not crazy to bid two hundred and sixty.

Auction is proven. Keeneland™ Thoroughbred Horse Auctions, Barrett Jackson Auto Auctions™, Sotheby's® fine art, our own real estate auctions happen routinely, daily, weekly, monthly, year after year because they work. When companies specialize in a particular type of product and conduct thousands of those sales, they improve their processes, their people, and their clientele just by doing good business.

# CHAPTER 6

## AUCTION AS A STRATEGY

If you're a buyer, the strategy behind auction is primal. It's about the dread of loss and the excitement of opportunity. We all love nightly news stories about the guy who went to an auction and bought a dime-store print, peeled the back off the frame, and found he'd bought a Van Gogh, proving that one man's trash is another man's treasure.

I remember the first time I placed a bid on eBay®. It was absolutely thrilling. I ran to the frig, made myself a sandwich, and came back fifteen minutes later to see if anyone had outbid me. In the beginning I bought small things just to make sure they'd actually arrive and look precisely as they were described. Then I graduated to more expensive items and finally cheered on my friends as they bought computers, expensive jewelry, and all manner of luxury items. I got comfortable with the idea that I might be outbid or that I could be ousted for anything from insufficient funds in my PayPal™ account to simply not abiding by the rules.

Then came the sniping software, the competing buyers' strategy that leapt onto eBay® in the last few seconds and ripped from my grasp the retro cowboy shirt I'd fought for all week. The computer screen named me the winner and then, instantly, I wasn't. Infuriating!

Whether it's shirts online or homes on the lawn, buyers have strategies. Ironically, sellers rarely do.

Why *don't* you have a real strategy for selling your home? Ask a friend about her "sales strategy" and she'll say, "Well, I thought I'd list it when the kids are out of school." That's like asking the Pittsburgh Steelers for their game day strategy and hearing, "We're going to get on the bus for the stadium." Not to underestimate the importance of showing up, but it's hardly a strategy.

**To develop a strategy, you have to know what you want from the sale.**

1.  **You want your home sold quickly.** If that's not true…
    if you're putting your home on the market but you're
    "in no hurry to sell," that's code for "I'm going to price
    it to make sure it *doesn't* sell." You're most likely listing
    it to please your spouse or find out what it might sell for
    if you ever got serious about selling.

2.  **You'd love more than one offer.** You pray for a bidding war where several people simultaneously try to buy your home and the offers keep escalating. (If you haven't had an offer in nearly a year, the odds of three people simultaneously making escalating offers on your house would be like a small lotto win.)

3.  **You want buyers with cash or financing in place.** You don't want someone at your open house to beam at you and announce, "I want to buy your house as soon as I sell mine, and we're almost sure our home will sell quickly. We're cleaning it up now and it will be on the market in six weeks." That's equivalent to someone saying, "I'll be over to buy your house just as soon as I'm hit by a moon rock."

4.  **You want motivated buyers.** Some people aren't buyers. They're just lonely and you're a free amusement park or literal chat room. Others have nothing to do but wander through open houses to get ideas about how to redecorate theirs. You want people who want to own a home… preferably by sundown.

5.  **You want to make plans, not contingencies.** Contingency conversations go on constantly in sellers' heads and sound something like this: "Well, if it sells by

43

August, we'll be okay because the schools don't start until September. If it sells by October, we're in good shape, but if it gets to be the holidays, the family is flying in, and I don't know what we'll do. Maybe we'll take if off the market till spring. It's got to sell by spring, everyone buys then, and, if it does, I won't have to pay the lawn service all summer."

6. **You want to know what day your home will sell.** Your real estate agent can't tell you what day your home will sell. Your auctioneer can. If you're taking a job in another city and need to get there in a few weeks, simply pack and depart, confident your home will be sold. But what about that old warning that you should leave your furniture in the house to keep it from looking so bare? Believe me, the new buyer doesn't need your couch to figure out where hers should go.

7. **You want to stop being held hostage by your house.** If the average house listed with a real estate agent stays on the market 225+ days before it sells, and the average auctioned home sells in thirty days, you just got seven months of your life back. Time is all we've got. Spending it in the right place, with the right people,

on the right issues is important. Auction can improve your quality of life.

8. **You want a quick close.** Real estate agents have lots of war stories about what goes on at the closing table, including buyers trying to renegotiate their deal. Life is full of surprises, and the closing on your house shouldn't be one of them.

9. **You want to preserve your property's reputation.** Failure to preserve the property's, the seller's, and the auction company's reputation costs a lot more than money.

A bank foreclosed on The Manor House, an historic old mansion nestled amid magnolia trees for a century. The local coffee shops buzzed with conversation about finding a new owner for the place.

A local businessperson made an offer to buy the mansion, which was now boarded up, but the bank rejected the offer saying it was too low. (Elsa Lewis, WWM's Exec VP of REO sales, reminds me that banks have their rejection reasons—write-downs too steep or ill timed, pressure from upstream investors, government breathing down their neck on every sale to see if they're abiding by all the new regulations.)

Almost two years later, the bank decided to auction the home.

The same person showed up and became the high bidder, but this time the offer was lower because the property needed a great deal of repair. The bank rejected the high bid.

The reputational backlash is clearly that the high bidder may never stop telling everyone he meets about his experience with the bank, the auction company, and the property. The auction company looks foolish for holding an auction in which the reserve was obviously far above current market value. The property is now in print as a forlorn, deteriorating asset that needs work. Do you think the property will *ever* bring more at a future sale?

**Auction is the sales strategy that meets your objectives.**

1. Your home will be auctioned thirty days from listing.
2. Many bidders will have the opportunity to compete for your home.
3. The high bidder has to have cash or his financing in place.
4. Buyers are motivated because the sale is time definite.
5. You make plans, not contingencies—move out and on with your life.
6. You can pick the day you want your property to sell.
7. You can stop being held hostage by your home.
8. You can close the deal thirty days after the auction or in

just a few days with Quick Close™, which means you pay the buyer's closing costs in exchange for an immediate cash deal.

9.   You avoid any speculation about your property's condition and value.

Auction is a powerful sales strategy. So if you're still thinking of just listing your real estate and waiting for a buyer to show up, remember the age-old definition of insanity: "Doing the same thing over and over again but expecting different results."

47

# CHAPTER 7

## COMFORT FOR CONTROL FREAKS

When I first started raising horses, I believed I controlled my twelve-hundred-pound mount with the two little leather reins, until the day I rode him into a high wind and a flock of fifty geese flushed from the ground in front of us, filling the air with a cacophony of squawking and flapping. My horse's immediate response was a fast 360 and a sudden halt, a jarring reminder that helped me formulate my definition of control: a temporary meeting of the minds that can become completely unhinged when panic ensues.

It's natural instinct that the more frightening the world becomes, the more we try to protect our interests through control. Ironically the more stringent our controls, the more we expose ourselves to failure.

China's government provides a good illustration. In their attempt to stave off a population explosion, they instituted the one-child-per-family dictate or, more plainly, population control, the results of which were documented in several articles, including one in a 2005 edition of *The New England Journal of Medicine*. Faced with only one child per family, the urban Chinese chose to keep boy babies because they would grow up to become providers. A decade later, China realized they had no teenage girls to care for the elderly, and more edicts followed to control that crisis with a second-baby approval system under certain rigid conditions, creating more havoc and a growing black market for ways couples could keep their children. According to a report by China's State Population and Family Planning Commission, China will have thirty million more men than women in 2020 and may be importing brides.

Increasingly greater control created events that became out of control. To quote *The New England Journal of Medicine*, "The shortage of women may have increased mental health problems and socially disruptive behavior among men and has left some men unable to marry and have a family. The scarcity of females has resulted in kidnapping and trafficking of women for marriage and increased numbers of commercial sex workers, with a potential resultant rise in human immunodeficiency virus infection and other sexually trans-mitted diseases."

This same kind of control can be seen in our own country with the current housing crisis. Government didn't want to release too many foreclosed homes into the marketplace, accept prices that were too low, or allow people to buy and then flip houses for a profit. They didn't want people who wouldn't agree to live in the home. They didn't want people removed from their homes. They didn't want any number of things and so they took control, managing who bought, when, where, how, and for how much.

Never has government spent so much time and money trying to control the free market with such disastrous results. Loan mods, re-mods, principal write-downs, tax incentives, discounted closing costs, and free appliances at closing have done nothing to unclog the foreclosure pipeline. (In fact, I'm hard-pressed to name a government program that's ever "sped things up.") Today, homes can be in some stage of foreclosure for two years, while the house rots, the copper is stolen, and the owner has long gone. Government is now proposing we turn mortgage bankers into landlords. In August of 2011, the Associated Press reported, "The Obama administration may turn thousands of government-owned foreclosures into rental properties to help boost falling home prices." And the latest last-ditch effort at control is, according to the *Wall Street Journal,* a bipartisan bill that "would give residence visas to foreigners who spend at least $500,000 to buy houses in the U.S." For all the government-control measures, things are decidedly out of control in the housing arena.

All of which brings us back to you and me, trying to control our own little piece of the planet—our personal real estate trans-action—and attempting to force the marketplace to pay our asking price rather than allowing people to compete openly for our home. The price you pay for "price control" is expensive in terms of carrying costs (mortgage payments, taxes, upkeep), net present value of money, lost opportunity to purchase something else or *do* something else, and years stolen from your life.

Auction puts you *more* in control of your sale than any other selling method. Here are a few of the things you can manage and control:

1. **Research and selection of the auction company.**

   • **Ask NAA, the National Auctioneers Association in Overland Park, Kansas for a list of real estate auctioneers across the country.** (Go to www.auctioneers.org.) As with any industry trade organization, an auction company doesn't have to be expert or the best in their field to join, but they are expected to maintain good business practices. The NAA has a long code of ethics, and articles 1 and 2 state: "Members pledge to lawfully and ethically promote the interests of the seller." And "Members owe the buyer the duties

of honesty, integrity and fair dealing at all times."
(Williams & Williams® is a long-standing member
and supporter of NAA.)

- **Test-drive the buyer experience.** Various auction
  companies conduct real estate auctions every month.
  The auction locations and dates will be posted on
  the companies' Web sites. Plan to attend one of their
  auctions and determine if it was conducted profes-
  sionally, if terms and conditions of the sale were
  clearly stated, questions from the crowd answered,
  and the auctioneer helpful and skillful at selling.

- **Ask the high bidder.** Find out from the high bidder
  if you could contact him after closing to see how
  happy he was with the process. A lot of times
  the event can appear to be a great sale and then the
  property never closes. Remember, the auction is only
  *half* of the event. The closing is the important second
  half. A top-ranked closing department is just as important as a top-ranked auctioneer—they bookend
  the two sides of the sale.

- **Talk to the seller.** Find out if he or she was pleased
  with the way the auction company performed.

- **Evaluate the care factor.** Find out how the auction

53

company has handled customer complaints and litigation. No company is perfect, but you want to find out if they're continually striving to be.

- **Track good press and bad.** Ask the company to address negative press comments. Check the Internet for the company's press and, if you find something odd, ask your auction sales rep about it. Even the way he answers your question will tell you a lot about the company. For example, if all the complaints against the company are due to "a crazy seller" you might want to think twice before becoming the next one.

2.  **Understand the ground rules before signing a contract.**

- Don't assume anything. No question is too trivial. Get the answers that make you comfortable.

- Ask the auction company to spell out everything, from the listing agreement all the way to closing.

- Understand how you've agreed to sell your property: e.g. with reserve, Absolute, or with an assured sales price. We will discuss this in Chapter Nineteen.

3.  **Meet the team.**

- Who will be the executives assigned to your sale? Can you reach them at all times on their cell phones

or do you have to wait for business hours and go
through the switchboard?

4.   **Ask for a detailed marketing plan.**

- **How much will they spend, where, and why?**
  Do they mass-market or target-market, and against
  what demographic and psychographics?

- **How many open houses will be held?** How will they
  be manned? Are your personal belongings insured
  and protected, or do you have to remove them?

- **Does the auction company work with real estate
  agents?** Who pays the agent and what communication will take place between the auction company
  and the agent?

- **Know what you're expected to do or not do.**
  This varies by auction company. We don't encourage sellers to attend open houses because they can
  actually talk buyers out of coming to the auction
  without even knowing it. Something as innocent as,
  "I'm so glad you like the upstairs. So did my husband's mother. She died peacefully up there reading
  a book and we found her when we came home from
  a two-day vacation." Kind of takes the luster off the
  place, doesn't it?

5.   **Determine your downside risk and upside reward.**
Your personal needs and your pocketbook motivate you.
The auction company should be motivated by its reputation. (Because auction is such a public activity, auction
companies can't afford too many failed sales.) The mutual
goal is to sell the property at the highest possible market
value and have a successful closing.

- **Set a reasonable reserve.** The reserve is the value
  the auction company must achieve at auction
  or the seller has the right not to sell. The reserve
  should be intellectually and analytically reasonable.
  The value should be based on recent auctions and
  reliable data from traditional sales, as well as the
  auction company's knowledge of the property and
  the area. Remember that setting an unrealistic
  reserve keeps the house unsold and gives the home,
  the seller, and the auction company a reputation for
  toying with buyers and conducting sales for properties that never change hands.

- **Discuss upfront marketing money.** Demonstrate
  that you are going to sell the home by setting a low
  reserve or selling Absolute, meaning the property
  will sell to the highest bidder regardless of price.

In that way, you avoid upfront marketing fees to cover the auction company's marketing expenses, which are usually refundable at closing; or turndown fees, non-refundable if the seller rejects the high bid. Know the circumstances under which these monies are requested from you and credited back to you or refunded entirely.

6.  **Obtain milestone reports.**

    • **Know where you are in the marketing process.** When does the marketing break and where? When are photos taken and open houses scheduled?

    • **Are potential buyers being reached?** Obtain a report from the auction company tracking sign placement, Web hits, e-mail responses, phone calls, bid deposits, and open-house attendees. Ask how your property is performing compared to other similar properties they've sold in the same geographic area. If it's not performing well, what do they do to improve market response?

7.  **Communicate & cooperate with your auction company.**

    • **Do they want you to talk to potential buyers?** When you insert yourself between the auction company and the buyer, you can negatively impact the high bid. You would be surprised how many sellers on auction day tell a registered bidder, "Well, if we got two hundred and fifty thousand at this point, we'd be delighted!" They've just informed the potential buyer that he shouldn't plan to bid above that amount and he could most likely get it for less, because that statement has a tone of desperation.

- **Share your personal story.** The story behind the purchase of the home you're now selling needs to be communicated to the auction company and perhaps even shared in the marketing. If a young couple learns your family lived happily in this home for three generations, they might feel good about starting their family in the same place.

- **Share the history of your property.** We all like to know the history—whether the house was home to a mobster or simply has friendly ghosts in the attic. Believe it or not, you never have to hide the strangeness of a place. There's someone for every property!

# Compare Your Control with Auction Versus Traditional Sales

| WILLIAMS & WILLIAMS REAL ESTATE AUCTION | FOR SALE BY OWNER OR REAL ESTATE AGENT |
|---|---|
| You pick the date your property sells | Buyer decides when to make offer |
| You decide when your property closes | Buyer negotiates closing date |
| Carrying costs limited to average 30 days | Costs go on indefinitely until sale |
| Buyers compete in open competition | Buyers have no reason to compete |
| Auction sales are "as is where is" | Buyers negotiate contigencies |
| Auctioneer wants to sell your home | Agent wants to sell any home |
| Auction delivers buyer in 30 days | 2011 average days on market 225+ |
| Reaches national, state and local buyers | Agent delivers local market |
| Live bidding on lawn with remote national & global bidding | Contracts from individuals come through the agent |
| Close 95% of approved offers | Closing rates unknown |

You control your home auction through *research* (determining if you're right for auction and, if so, which auction company is right for you), through *communication* (sharing all the information about your property and your personal needs surrounding the sale), and by *monitoring* (tracking each step of your auction by staying in touch with your auction team).

By choosing auction, you also control your personal time, energy, and money, and the sale of your house in thirty days. You haven't exercised this much control since you refused a second dip of Ben & Jerry's® Cherry Garcia™.

# CHAPTER 8

## OWN WHO YOU ARE AND SELL WHAT YOU OWN

If you're like many sellers, you think only certain types of real estate are "right" for auction, when in fact it's just the opposite. *All* real estate is right for auction, but all sellers aren't.

When it comes to secrets, sellers have them, and it's surprising how they can impact a sale, beginning with your relationship to the community, other family members, and the property itself.

### YOUR RELATIONSHIP TO THE COMMUNITY:

Are you a community leader or the guy in the neighborhood who tells kids to "get away from my house!" Are you "lights out by nine" or does the fun begin when the Chippendale® boys pull up in the driveway? Is your front yard tastefully landscaped or covered in so much statuary that it's often mistaken for a shrine?

Your neighbors know who you are, what you have, and what goes on at your house. And if they don't know, they surmise it. (Why do you think police officers interview neighbors about a suspect?)

If the neighbors like you, they want you to do well in life, and that includes selling your house at auction. If they dislike you, they don't want you to make a nickel and in rare instances conspire to make that happen during the auction. This is true whether you're selling your residence or your investment property.

We auctioned a beautiful hotel chain in the Northwest, a group of pristine properties filled with expensive antiques. An Internet search on this particular seller would only have revealed what was seemingly obvious...he was a prominent, wealthy, and influential person in the community. He was, in addition, a fairly congenial client wanting to rid himself of a large portfolio of real estate assets only because he wanted to re-invest in others.

We marketed the properties across the country and around the globe, and day of sale, the sales site was packed with people. When the bidding began, it was quickly evident from the furtive glances and scowling faces that few registered bidders intended to buy, and many looked as if they'd only shown up hoping for a train wreck.

We sold one property and delayed the other sales until we could have a private conversation with the seller, who finally admitted he hadn't won any popularity contests in the city. Internet blogging and newspaper coverage accused him of everything from negligence to simply heartless cruelty.

How successful do you think the townspeople wanted this seller to be? Had he confided his reputation in the community, he would have sold his real estate at a higher value because the structure of that auction, including where we held it, how we marketed it, and even how we addressed the crowd would have been entirely different.

It might have been as simple as the auctioneer saying, "Ladies and gentlemen, we know that some of you are here today for a fabulous real estate sale and others of you are here in hopes the seller won't do very well at this auction. But one thing is certain, when this sale is over the seller will be gone and you will be the new owner of this beautiful property and will have the opportunity to care for the asset and the community."

The audience and bidders simply want their concerns acknowledged, and once that happens, they can proceed to bid. Auction companies have to remind themselves that just because someone is prominent, wealthy, or ensconced in the community, he isn't necessarily embraced or supported by it. The rich don't have fewer secrets than the poor; they merely have more places to hide them.

Fortunately, more often than not the seller is liked and perhaps will even be missed by his community or neighborhood, and the auctioneer should note that fact as well, not only to honor the seller but to keep the bidders from believing if they bid on the seller's property they are somehow "taking something" from a person they like and respect.

The auctioneer needs a strong skill set, a talented team, and the ability to win the seller's trust. Without trust, you'll tell the auctioneer that you're selling because you just need a little extra cash rather than saying your wife left you and cleaned out your bank account or your neighbor has threatened your life, or your siblings are at war over the trust you manage for the family.

All of these issues affect the sale and therefore they will inevitably surface during the auction process. If they surface early, you may suffer a little awkwardness in revealing them; however, the auction company can then help you. If they surface late, they can cost you lost opportunity and revenue.

YOUR RELATIONSHIP TO THE REAL ESTATE YOU'RE SELLING:
In addition to understanding your relationship to your neighbors and the community, we have to know your relationship to your real estate. That relationship, incorrectly assessed, can be highly unrewarding for everyone involved.

We received a call from an investor in Nevada who had hundreds of properties across the US. Over the years she had failed to pay the taxes on them. Now the government was going to seize the properties to pay the tax bills. The problem seemed straightforward—sell the assets and pay the taxes.

During the auction, the auctioneer discovered that the woman had an ex-boyfriend bidding on the assets with the intention of failing to close, in order to return the assets to her. Aside from blocking his ability to bid, we quizzed our client about her extremely odd plan. She was going to lose her properties for back taxes, so why have a phantom bidder try to win, not close, and give them back to her? What was she thinking?

Finally, after some probing, she admitted to being a hoarder—unable to separate herself from her belongings. Many people who suffer from this affliction can barely make their way through their house to get to their bed. While they may have good jobs and dress neatly, their home may be littered with everything from garbage bags, broken appliances, paper and plastic, to animal feces. If we had understood her relationship to her assets, we would have known that a woman who's unable to separate herself from her Walmart® sacks could never separate herself from her real estate. In fact, as the closing neared, she developed health issues due to the stress of "letting go." To her credit, she overcame that stress and was finally able to release those pieces of her life.

Contrast this with another of our sellers who had their home on the market for a year and, when it didn't sell, took a friend's advice and rented it so they could move out of state. Being a long-distance landlord became a burden, so they decided not to renew the rental agreement. The renter refused to leave and they had to evict him. After many more months, the house was finally empty again and now needed repairs. The sellers' relationship with their home was simple—they wanted it to end!

During a trip to get the house in shape, they attended a WW auction and subsequently contacted DC Roberts, our head of Distinctive Properties. Thirty days later she phoned them from the driveway of their home to say the auction had just ended and we'd delivered 150 percent of their reserve. In their words, "We are waay beyond happy—we're euphoric!"

### Your Personal Needs Surrounding the Sale:

Whether small investor or individual seller, anyone who sells their real estate usually experiences some degree of emotional loss, even if the sale is accompanied by financial gain. Despite the fact that you may say you'll be glad to get rid of the responsibility of the house or the business or family farm, when it comes to letting go, emotions surface. Maybe you're selling something you don't want to give up but can no longer afford. Or you're selling something you know you *need* to give up but you're still attached to it in some way. Or you're selling something you can't wait to get rid of but you feel less than brilliant for having bought it in the first place.

To allow yourself to move on, you have to get something from the sale that satisfies an emotional need. That emotional need is very hard for any seller to articulate, because it makes you seem vain or perhaps overly sentimental or too selfish or a dozen other things you'd prefer not to share. Inevitably the emotional need is far more complex than simply achieving a particular sales price. If you don't know what you need from the sale, or you know but you won't articulate it, how can the auction company ever deliver it? You believe you're just cleaning up old karma with the sale of your house or selling off the responsibilities that have been weighing you down for years or perhaps just moving to a smaller place now that the kids are grown. You haven't taken time to consider what has to happen for you to feel this sale was a good decision.

In addition to the monetary proceeds from the sale, what do you want? A celebratory farewell, an honoring of a lifetime spent, an acknowledgement of your good taste, or something else? And what would have to happen before, during, or after the auction for you to celebrate positive closure to that part of your life?

One woman requested that we auction her home in the backyard rather than the front, so that if her ex-husband showed up, he'd see that the cab of his classic '54 Chevy™, in which she'd caught him with

67

another woman, had been turned into a greenhouse and the truck bed a birdbath. On the inside roof of the cab, visible only if you were in a reclining position in the front seat, she'd scrawled, "If you're reading this, you're already gone." Her auction, by the way, was a great success.

# CHAPTER 9

## EVERY SELLER HAS A BUFFALO

Tommy Williams tells the story about selling a ranch that belonged to a fellow from West Texas named Sam. He was a very entrepreneurial gentleman whose career in banking and the entertainment business was legendary—many a billionaire had gotten his very first business loan from this show-biz banker. Now in his nineties, Sam saw only his personal assistant, Mary, whom he asked to contact Williams & Williams about selling his ranch.

He believed in auction and, in this case, wanted to sell with reserve. Tommy agreed and asked Eric Johnson, who today leads our Farm & Ranch division, to manage the auction.

Sam had Mary drive him out to the ranch, where Sam got behind the wheel of an old pickup and gave Eric a high-speed, terrifying tour of the property. They whipped across the flat, dry prairie, bounced over the occasional hill, and narrowly missed tree groves, giving Eric a microscopic fly-by of weathered tree bark. Suddenly Sam screeched the truck to a halt alongside a heavy pipe fence and whistled. A massive old bull buffalo came running full speed at the vehicle and jammed its nose into the open window. Sam chuckled as he picked up some oranges off the floorboard of the truck and began hand-feeding the old bull. Such a primitive beast that could have crushed them in a hoof-beat came to eat fresh fruit from his hand. Sam said he hoped that the bull he called Homer and the twenty female buffalo would find a good home after the auction. Eric didn't think too much about Sam's remark. Many of our auction team members have spent a lifetime in the cattle business, said good-bye to prize Angus bulls, and understood there was always a sadness surrounding it.

That evening, Tommy and Eric laid out their plan for parceling and selling the real estate. They decided when it came to the buffalo, they'd round them up like cattle the morning of the sale.

Auction day dawned beautiful and sunny as the crowds gathered in the pastures of this well-marketed full-dispersal sale. (Full dispersal is a term used most often in conjunction with a farm or ranch sale in which not only the real estate, but also the livestock, farm equipment, and personal items are sold as well.) Sam had gotten weaker over the past three weeks and was unable to attend the sale, but he eagerly awaited the results by phone.

Everyone in the large crowd seemed happy and excited for the auction to begin except Eric, who looked more wild-eyed than the buffalo as he muttered that he thought Homer had taken a personal dislike to him. The big, wooly animal had broken out of the corral three times since daybreak.

Minutes before the auction, as if to verify Eric's remarks, there was a horrific crash and Homer broke out again, this time destroying the corral and leading the herd away from the sale site. Eric jumped into a vehicle to pursue the buffalo and seconds later flew past the busted corral faster than anyone knew an RTV could travel. Homer thundered behind him, at full throttle, wearing the sixteen-foot corral gate on his horns, like a demented Carmen Miranda, determined to flatten Eric with it. A fellow in attendance to bid on the buffalo shouted, "You folks ain't sold a lotta buffalo, I take it. Shoulda put tar paper around the corral. If a buffalo can *see* out, he'll *get* out."

Tommy announced that the buffalo looked like a healthy, energetic herd and they would be sold subject to the buyer being able to corral them within twenty-four hours of becoming the high bidder. The crowd laughed and the auction began.

The ranch land, ranch house, all the equipment, and the cattle brought far more than Sam had hoped. Tommy and Eric couldn't wait to tell him the good news. "The ranch brought three times your reserve price!"

Sam seemed almost uninterested. "What did Homer sell for?" he asked. When Eric told him the price was $1000, Sam went silent. How could that gentle old male buffalo have been so unappreciated? He was heartsick that Homer had sold for so little.

"Now remember," Tommy said in relaying the story, "we're talking about a *gigantic,* old male buffalo who can flat-foot a pipe fence. It's not just everyone with a place to put him!" He stopped smiling. "The problem is that we never bothered to sincerely brag on him."

The old bull buffalo wasn't prize worthy or monetarily valuable, but Sam and the buffalo had been through a lot together and he loved him. Throughout the marketing and into the auction, Sam never said very much about the buffalo, and therefore no one had acknowledged the relationship or praised the buffalo, other than to sell him as requested.

Like all ranching coming to an end, the rancher rightfully wanted public recognition for his life's work—but, more so, recognition for Homer. The auction team had mistakenly believed the sale was about delivering Sam top dollar, missing the fact that dollars weren't what Sam needed as much as a home where his buffalo could roam and receive recognition for his gentle beauty.

Most likely that large animal, who was always standing there when Sam returned to the ranch ready to greet him, epitomized everything the rancher had created on that piece of ground and in his business life. Sam's need had nothing to do with money achieved at auction and everything to do with the buffalo. Had we acknowledged the specialness of the buffalo, called local zoos, animal refuges, or other ranches and found a place where Sam could have donated Homer and then visited him, we would have met his needs. Had we told the story of the buffalo in the newspaper so he could have shown the picture to his friends at the assisted-living facility, the sale would have been a huge success, regardless of what the real estate brought him monetarily.

Every seller has a buffalo. The smart auction company finds it early and treats it with respect. Unless the buffalo is honored, no sale can ever be a success.

Today, we sell many ranches every month, recently a 1200-acre cow calf operation. The sale was another full dispersal. We knew the seller because we'd sold him a portion of this same ranch years ago, and now it was time to resell it. He called us because he liked the way we'd handled the sale the first time around. The seller had been a minister before he became a rancher. Now he believed he was being called back to the ministry.

We had forty auction staff at the sale, which included the acreage, several homes, rows of heavy equipment, and a herd of Black Angus. Despite the fact that record heat hit Oklahoma for more than fourteen days and this particular day the temperature at sale time had cooled down to 107 degrees in the shade, more than eight hundred people showed up and stood out in the sun to buy. The thirty acres reserved for parking wasn't enough. The lines in front of the concession stands were long, and water was being handed out by the tub-full.

At ten a.m., some of the finest auctioneer families in the country—the Williams, the Lowdermans, and the Heldermans, led by Tommy Williams—were ready to sell land and equipment in choreographed order. First the farmhouses and ranch land. People walked to the equipment area where rows of tractors, tillers, and bailers were auctioned, then on to look at the cattle and indoors to bid on them with Tom Burke, leading sales manager for Angus cattle, and Steve Dorran, a top-notch cattle auctioneer. The well-orchestrated five-million-dollar auction was an all-day, old-fashioned, bring-the-family event, except for the fact that it was streamed live on Auction Network® and clerked electronically.

But that description isn't what the auction was about, as we'd come to learn over the years. This auction was a life transition—from rancher to minister.

When the cowboys gathered inside the small arena, seated on bleachers or standing next to them, and before the cattle auctioneer was ready to start, the seller took the microphone to explain what he was doing and why he was selling. He blessed all the cowboys and the cattle they were buying and then said a prayer as each man removed his hat and held it over his heart in respect. And with that, the seller, head bowed, walked from the arena, having blessed the land before leaving it.

Needless to say, the sale itself was a complete success because *every* aspect of the seller's needs had been met. It didn't matter whether the auction attendees were religious or atheist, whether the auction company had orchestrated what happened or just participated in it, because it wasn't about any of us. It was about the seller and his need, which in this case was to say good-bye in a way that held meaning for *him*. The buffalo had been honored.

# CHAPTER 10

## CHANGING YOUR FEAR OF CHANGE

The famous 1967 Holmes and Rahe Stress Scale measured human stress levels for everything from moving to a new home, landing a new job, getting married or divorced, having a baby, experiencing the death of a family member to simply taking a vacation or receiving a promotion. Regardless of whether the change was sorrowful or celebratory, the individual experienced stress when he attempted to adjust to his new condition.

Stressful situations often trigger the need for auction. A parent dies and you have to part with the family home; divorce occurs and you no longer want to live in the house. Parenthood creates a need for a home with more bedrooms, while a surprise promotion requires a move to a new city. Auction is sometimes associated with a stressful life event, when in fact it's the bridge to a new beginning.

Auction companies know that individual sellers, under stress, can go nuclear over the strangest issues. One seller insisted just before the auction that he wanted to take his bathtub with him. He did all his creative thinking in the tub and decided if he left it, he might never create again. Removing a bathtub is no small matter, particularly if it's twenty-four hours before the auction. Fortunately we were able to convince him to take a large potted plant instead so that his creativity could blossom elsewhere.

If you look forward to change, you'll love auction. If change scares you, you're not alone. Not only individuals but even cities have difficulty with change. A classic example was our auctioning of the Silverdome. Despite the dome being on the market for seven years, and Pontiac, Michigan in near bankruptcy, nothing was changing until the governor appointed an emergency funds manager—and that decisive change caused all hell to break loose. Some people will fight to their death to stop change—even if lack of change could mean their demise.

As I told *DS News* in April following the sale, the auction of the Silverdome was over in seconds. The Canadian bidder was the new owner of the Pontiac Silverdome for $583,000. We knew the auction had been a success. The press and the rest of the world, however, debated, broadcasted, and blogged, lamenting that the dome was worth far more. After all, the Detroit Lions®' legendary playing field had originally cost more than $50 million to build back in 1975.

"The Silverdome is worth millions, and this is a disgrace" was the resounding response, but the dissident voices hadn't shown up at the auction cash in hand, to pay even slightly more in order to prove their point.

Fred Leeb, Michigan's state-appointed emergency financial manager, faced hard facts when he hired us. The dome hadn't been occupied since 2002. Traditional brokers had worked diligently for the past three years trying to sell it, while the city had paid roughly $12 million in holding costs and was facing another $1.5 million annually just to keep the ten-acre, 200-ton roof inflated. Unoccupied, the 132-acre, 80,325-seat dome situated in a city struggling with serious financial problems in economically hard-hit Michigan contributed no tax dollars, no new jobs, and not a modicum of entertainment.

The governor had tapped Leeb for solutions. It was mid-October 2009, and by year's end the city would be out of money to support the dome. An auction company that could manage something of this scope had to be found, the deal negotiated, the dome listed, marketed, auctioned, and closed by December 31—all in roughly seventy-two days.

After choosing Williams & Williams®, Leeb agreed to sell "Absolute," meaning if the dome brought a dollar, that's what it would sell for. Absolute sales are a signal to buyers that, regardless of previous failed attempts to sell an asset, they can bid with confidence because this time the asset will be trading hands with integrity. Not rejected or renegotiated, but sold to the highest bidder.

Our executive team weighed the risks to our reputation and the political fallout of taking the dome to auction. Tommy Williams shouted, "Do you know how many people need a dome in this economy? If I gave you the keys to the dome today and said it's yours for free and all you have to do is pay $1.5 million annually to keep it inflated, pay the taxes, utilities, staff, repairs, and maintenance, what would you do with it? When you take on something like this, it's not about the money. It's your reputation that's at stake above everything else." Having reviewed the downside, we planned for success.

We marketed the Silverdome globally across two hundred countries and territories, and investors from eighty-four of those made inquiries. We had teams of commercial sales execs fielding calls from around the world, vetting financial viability, and helping prepare a wide variety of bidders for the day of the auction.

And on Monday, November 16, 2009, at one p.m. EST, when Tommy Williams stood before the room of spectators and bidders in Pontiac, the market spoke. A thirty-five-year-old deserted dome in Michigan was worth $583,000. Even nostalgic memories of Barry Sanders roaring down the field didn't change that. Leeb congratulated us and told the gasping press that Williams & Williams® had accomplished expertly what the city had asked. The Canadian buyer, whom no one had yet met in person, stated by phone that he was planning to bring professional soccer teams to the United States. But who was he? And would he really? And how had a "foreigner" waltzed off with the dome?

Pontiac was awash in vociferous opinions. A city councilor expressed anger over the low sales price. Others said it didn't matter because the buyer would never close. An enraged citizenry filed a class-action lawsuit that was judicially dismissed a few days later. The Silverdome sale made the 2009 B-list of business blunders, and late-night comedy included it alongside Goldman Sachs™ and the Congressional recess as "Things Not to Be Thankful for." All the while, Leeb, and the state of Michigan, stood tall. The market had spoken even more loudly and with greater clarity than the clamor around their decision to auction the dome. The real estate bubble might have fallen, collapsing on Pontiac, but the dome would stay inflated.

Within days Dan Falls, who leads our Commercial team, received calls from owners of other massive buildings in Michigan and the surrounding area saying privately what they didn't want to voice publicly: Williams & Williams® had gotten what the dome was worth, and they wanted to sell their property too.

The Silverdome closed on schedule on December 29, 2009. Two months later, we heard from the city of Pontiac. Leeb reported that the Silverdome had "hundreds of people in there working, cleaning, fixing, and bringing it up to date. The new owner hired the local police force for security during events. Two international rock stars were booked for a concert. Four soccer teams are scheduled to compete this spring. This new owner is the true needle-in-the-hay-stack, miracle buyer."

As the press gingerly reported that the dome appeared to be off life support and looking a lot healthier, one lone blogger wrote that he couldn't believe the new owner intended to fill the dome with soccer teams that people had "never heard of," demonstrating inexorably what your mother taught you: You can't please everyone.

Leeb and the state of Michigan saw a problem and said we have to fix this. It can't get better unless we take action. No one will save us but ourselves. Leeb's concerns, as well as the citizens' of Michigan, were those of everyone who owns real estate and doesn't want to: what's the property worth?

Whether it's REO (the acronym for Real Estate Owned by a bank), commercial, farms, estates, bulk sales, or the Silverdome, what's it worth? We have a sophisticated analytics department whose life is dedicated to the Holy Grail of determining what any piece of real estate on the planet will bring at any given moment; our models, matrixes, and proprietary mathematical formulas excite investors and encourage clients. But in truth, no one can predict unequivocally what every asset is worth. The litmus test for valuation is the moment when the evaluator writes you a check to back up his number.

If assets are marketed robustly, intelligently, and even globally, and buyers are psychographically and demographically targeted, and they log in, tune in, show up, and then all stop bidding at a given number, how can one argue that the asset was worth more? It's like standing on the trading floor of the New York Stock Exchange™ at four thirty p.m. shouting, "Stop! Google® is worth much more!"

Had Pontiac placed a "value" on the Silverdome, they would still own it. Instead the property has a new steward and the dome's "net" via auction exceeds any artificial valuation. Now the dome creates new jobs, perhaps necessitates the reopening of restaurants and shops nearby, and kids attend games there and may be inspired to grow up to be athletes. The return on investment for Pontiac could end up being a new beginning.

Whether you're the seller of the Silverdome or the house on Silver Drive, you have to envision what life can be like on the other side of the sale and change what you're doing to get there.

# CHAPTER 11

## YOUR REAL ESTATE AGENT GENE

I sold my own country-club home at auction and the real estate agent from whom I'd purchased it was nearly apoplectic. Despite our having become friendly over the years, she was now clearly not speaking to me.

I'd listed it for six months and then decided to sell "For Sale By Owner." I'd created elaborate fliers, held open houses, and basically shown it to anyone breathing, all while maintaining a full-time job as president of a large media company. Why in the world would an executive of a major corporation become her own real estate agent? Because I was like all sellers—I believed my home was unique, gorgeous, a reflection of my perfect good taste: marble pillars, thirty-foot ceilings, massive windows in the sunroom overlooking dozens of giant oak trees in a backyard longer than center court at Wimbledon.

It was a home for parties and people. Never mind that I didn't like parties nor was I friends with enough people to ever appropriately populate the place. It was a trophy house, purchased because my CPA said I needed a bigger tax deduction and my ego said I needed a bigger status symbol.

When potential buyers with young children wandered through asking me if I knew how much it would cost to rip out the floor, or if carpet strips could be nailed to terrazzo, I went into visible spasms. They were worried that their children would run through the large living room, fall on the terrazzo, and crack open their heads like co-conuts, or that an elderly parent might do an involuntary triple lutz and die on the spot. I was worried only that I would never find "the right buyer"—the one who appreciated a work of art.

I needed a nice, young, wealthy couple with no children, or two gay men with great design taste who wanted to live in Oklahoma.

After a year of no such buyers, my masterpiece became a white elephant, and after another year it was a drain on my checkbook and quality of life. I decided to auction it!

On this chilly winter day, my former real estate agent swept across the lawn, her large black cape slicing Zorro-like through the wind as she warned the gathering crowd that this auction would bring "nothing," ruin home values, and disgrace the neighborhood. And yet, she knew the home well. She could have called me day or night and shown the home and I would gladly have paid her for bringing "the right buyer." Her frustration was most likely in knowing that *no buyer* would meet my needs or my asking price. And therein lies one of the reasons that real estate agents spread the word that auction is a horrible, tainting event that ruins home values. Auction accomplishes in thirty days what they've been trying to do for months or years. Auction forces potential buyers off the sidelines and makes them perform. It also makes sellers like me stop trying to control the market and allow the market to deliver value.

The auctioneer began the sale. The bidding was fast and then slowed as it neared $350K. The auctioneer reminded the crowd that this was the finest neighborhood in the city and the property was in pristine condition. The bidding began again and went to $400K, where it stalled. The auctioneer spoke again and the bidding went to $425K, then $430K, and crept up in increments of five thousand dollars until it stalled at $460K, where the auctioneer reminded the crowd of the values all around this home. Bidding then went up in thousand-dollar increments until it stopped at $467,000. The crowd had been driven to its limits. None of the high bidders would pay more than current market value, which today in this spot, at this time, with this home was $467,000. The high bid was slightly below my reserve and therefore I could reject it, refuse to sell, and keep my property. And $467K would not pay off my mortgages!

My mind raced. A lot of wealthy, engaged bidders were present at the auction, so the marketing had done its job. I had long ago pulled out $100K from the equity in the house to build pipe fencing on my ranch, so I'd increased the amount I owed the bank by borrowing against my house. I'd rejected offers for two years; everyone who could possibly have had an interest in it had seen it. I was driving back and forth every other day from my ranch to maintain this empty house—spending thousands of dollars a month on lawn service and mortgage payments. How long did I think I could continue? Holding on for two years had been torturous. I accepted the high bid. The agent walked past me and said loudly, "I could have gotten you *that!*"

The next day I made arrangements to take out a small loan, less than I owed on my automobile, to pay off the remaining mortgage. I was in shock. But I was also *relieved…* I could close this chapter in my life and move on to a better one.

As the days went by, I became inexplicably happier. I wasn't making the drive to maintain the house, and I felt freer than I had in a long time. Finally, months later, as I watched the sun rise over my ranch and the horses frolic in the cool air, I simply regretted that I'd wasted two years getting to my dream. I should have sold my city home at auction twenty-four months earlier and saved a lot of time and money. (I'll show you exactly how much in Chapter Seventeen.)

I thought about what the agent had said to me the day of the auction. Maybe she *could* have gotten me $467K, but she couldn't have let me see firsthand that's what my home was worth as bidders stood toe-to-toe competing for it.

I lived down the block from a family who had listed their home, sale pending, and then suddenly it was back on the market. Like everyone else in the neighborhood, I had begun to speculate. Was the busted sale on the house down the street due to the buyer, the seller, or problems with the home? Were those problems related to the creek that ran behind my house and was there something I should know? If so, the agent couldn't tell me.

And even if the sale of my neighbor's home went swimmingly and closed, I'd never know the real deal. I could find the official sales price, but what went into that sales price? Did the seller agree to finance? Did he leave the truck in the garage as an added incentive to close the deal? Did he agree to concessions like the furniture stays, the pool service will be paid for a year, the closing costs will be covered? The agent would have to keep that to herself and me in the dark.

We were all raised in a real-estate-agent-centric country. (Auctioneers are licensed real estate agents and brokers too.)

Your agent will suggest a list price and may even push back a bit if she feels you're pricing yourself out of the market, but if she pushes too hard she'll probably lose your listing. So she may say something like, "Well, let's go ahead and list at that price and see how it goes. We can always lower it later." She's allowed your hopes and wishes to supersede her skills, expertise, and knowledge.

Unfortunately, the bar is set low for real estate agents and auctioneers, and it has nothing to do with how much continuing education they take or how many tests they pass. That's why it's imperative that you do your homework before hiring either.

A real estate agent was thirty minutes late to show me a commercial building that she knew nothing about—not even how to turn the lights on or where the elevator was located. Our CFO took over and led her around. Relieved of her official duties, she trailed behind telling us this was getting to be a bad area and then regaled us with the owner's personal troubles. After that, she asked for our help in locking up the building and drove off, leaving us alone. I looked at my business associates and said, "So if we do this deal, do you think that was worth three percent?"

Contrast this with a local farm sale where bidders stood for hours in the sun waiting for the auctioneer to begin the real estate portion of the auction. The auctioneer rocked back in a chair under a shade tree, twirling a stick in his hand, and finally explained the delay to the exhausted crowd by shouting, "We'll get this y'here show on the road soon as I find my ring man. I'm bettin' he's inside gettin' hisself a big ole weenie!"

Unfortunate on both sides of the aisle, but at least you can spot these characters. More dangerous are the well-spoken, well-dressed agents and auctioneers who talk a great game but can't deliver.

Regardless, odds are that you'll call a real estate agent first because she's going to be more amenable to your comments about what your property is worth. Time is on her side. Time to let you acclimate to the market place, reject a few "low" offers before you realize your list price is too high. (Why do you think they call it last list? Because it's the last number listed before you lowered it again.)

Our company works with thousands of smart, motivated real estate agents. They understand that driving people around and discussing the quality of schools in the area is a thing of the past for many buyers.

Our policies vary depending on the type of property we're selling and on the client for whom we're selling it. In principle, we believe that everyone should pay the agent who represents them. Sellers should pay the listing agent if they want to keep them in the deal. Buyers should pay the buyer's agent if they need their help at the auction. Auction companies should pay the referring agent or broker who brought them the referral or client. If that were true, all agents would be paid by the person they represent and for whom they add value.

In August of 2011, NAR stated that for every two homes sold, an American job is created. If you line up all the people that new homeowners have to pay—remodelers, cement workers, painters, carpet layers, appliance installers, roofers, gardeners, landscapers, pool maintenance, and tree trimmers, to name a few—they might add up to one full-time human, so I agree.

In late 2010, real estate agents sold roughly 17 percent of the homes they listed each month. Auctioneers auctioned 100 percent of the homes they listed each month. So we believe hiring a real estate agent does put some people back to work...*and* hiring an auctioneer puts the entire country back on its feet!

# CHAPTER 12

## TAKE A DEEP BREATH AND SAY CURRENT MARKET VALUE

The most money any willing and able buyer will pay for a piece of real estate at this time, in this location, and under these circumstances defines current market value...the single most difficult concept for sellers to internalize.

You understand current market value as it relates to the current price of pork bellies or stocks on the exchange or even housing in general. But when it comes to trusting the market on that one asset you call home, the average person has a great deal of fear around the subject. Most often, you would rather incur the holding costs associated with a non-sale and struggle to find someone to agree with your asking price.

Think about the phrase "real estate holdings" as if it's hard to let go, or the phrase "holding costs," which is the cost of holding on. We should celebrate real estate "re-leasings." Let go, lease or release.

Mrs. Fields lived next door to her brother, whose home was identical to hers: both homes had the same floor plan, were built by the same builder in the same year, and were in the same condition.

After consulting with friends, she listed her home for a million dollars. One hundred days later, after little to no activity, she reduced her list price to $950K. On day 175 she lowered the price again to $900K. On day 200, her brother decided to sell his home by listing it for auction. Thirty days later, the high bidder at auction paid $850K. Immediately thereafter, Mrs. Fields received an offer for her home for $850K, which she accepted.

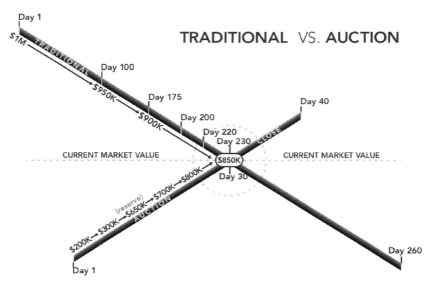

The process for the two houses is graphed on the previous page. The long line represents Mrs. Fields' home and the shorter line the auction of her brother's home. The auction line intercepted and ended the downhill slide of her last list price and her home's escalating days on market, demonstrating time wasted was quite simply money lost.

**Here are the take-aways from the sale of Mrs. Fields' home:**

1. Mrs. Fields wasted a great deal of time and money. Her holding costs included eight months of mortgage payments, maintenance, insurance, and taxes. Therefore her net was not $850K.

2. Mrs. Fields' home was over-priced from the very beginning, or she would have sold it for a million dollars.

3. She lowered the list price, signaling to potential buyers that she was admitting it was either over-priced or something was wrong with it.

4. She lowered the price again, signaling she was either desperate or something was definitely wrong with the house.

5. Her brother auctioned his home. The buying public watched current market value established openly

and honestly and, therefore, Mrs. Fields' home immediately sold for $850K as well.

6. Mrs. Fields "chased the market." She started at one million dollars when the market was most likely at $900K. A hundred days later, she dropped her price to $950K, but she still wasn't at market value, as evidenced by no offers to buy. By the time she'd lowered her price to $900K, the marketplace had dropped below that and she had over-exposed her home—everyone who might have been interested had already seen it and rejected it. She remained behind the marketplace throughout her marketing efforts.

7. Mrs. Fields tells the world selling her home was a "horrific, exhausting experience"...brought on by Mrs. Fields.

During the time sellers are lowering the list price and "keeping their fingers crossed," they inevitably tell the auction company that they *have* to get "that amount" of money when they sell "because that's what I have in it." Or they have to get that amount because "that's what I owe the bank."

That's akin to telling that great auction known as the New York Stock Exchange that on Monday morning you have to sell your Caterpillar stock for $150 dollars a share because that's what you paid for it. Your stock brings current market value, which is what *everything ultimately sells for.* And it's been proven that current market value is delivered more efficiently via auction.

In reaching current market value, real estate last-list prices start high and go down. Auction's opening bid starts low and goes up. It's simply a matter of whether you like up or down. Unless it's the number on my bathroom scales, I prefer up.

# CHAPTER 13

## GETTING THE MIDDLEMAN OUT OF THE MIDDLE

Middlemen are by and large disadvantageous in our society. There are exceptions. If you're being held hostage, you might welcome a negotiator, a middleman who, for a small fee and on your behalf, would speak to your captor and secure your release.

If the father of the young woman you want to marry has stated that he will shoot you on sight if you visit his daughter again, and therefore your showing up in person would clearly end your contribution to the gene pool, you might want a middleman, at some price, to speak on your behalf and smooth the relationship.

For centuries in certain circumstances, middlemen were not only desired but necessary—brokers of arranged marriages, military liaisons delivering messages between opposing camps, United Nations' translators, each performing a service the two disparate parties could not execute as well on their own. Events requiring middlemen seem to center around the danger or disadvantage of a face-to-face conversation or the inability to conduct one due to language barrier. But real estate transactions rarely fit either of those.

Today, we are a far more confident, courageous, and impatient people. Do you really need a loan broker who, for a small markup, goes back and forth between banks and gets the best loan rate for you, or can you get that on your own via the Internet or a few phone calls? Do you need a real estate agent to tell you the home is large and airy and perfect for a young family, or can you ascertain that yourself? Do you need an appraiser who measures and compares and tells you what the home is worth, or can you decide what the home is worth to you personally since you're the one writing the check?

Some of us clearly do need a middleman, and we pay for the privilege. Others of us decidedly do not and would like to save that time and money. Auction cuts out the middleman, which is why it frustrates or irritates so many people cued up in the middle of the real estate breadline. Why isn't an auctioneer just another middleman? Because he's doing something for you that you can't do yourself...drawing a crowd to compete for your home and selling it in thirty days.

You're assured from the time you're old enough to understand that purchasing a home is a critical decision, very bad things can happen, you can be "taken" or at the very least have to sue someone before it's all over. Experts, you're told, are there to guide and protect you. Auction, on the other hand, leaves it all up to you. Do you want guidance...if so how much and when? Do you need estimates, appraisals, opinions...you can order up as many as you want from whomever you want and at whatever cost.

You're driving by and you see the auction sign and with that information you begin your own due diligence. Some buyers do very little, and others go to the courthouse to check out the boundaries, invite structural engineers out to have a look at the weight-bearing walls, obtain estimates of what it would cost to fix the driveway or paint the outside. You can go online to comparative market sites like Trulia™ or Zillow® and find out what similar homes in that neighborhood have sold for, or look on the auction company's site to see what they've recently auctioned in that area. You might contact your banker or check your finances and decide what you're willing to spend, then go to the auction company's Web site and learn what items you need to take to the auction, like your checkbook and driver's license.

You attend the auction where the auctioneer reads the terms and conditions, answers questions, and the bidding begins. If you want the house, you raise your hand. If the bidding exceeds what you're willing to pay, you put your hand down. (No one ever buys a property by scratching his nose. If you made a mistake in bidding, quickly interrupt and say so. The auctioneer will back and up and correct the bidding.) You're in control. If you're the high bidder, you sign the contract and close in thirty days, or in only a few days if you're paying cash and the quick-close option is available. In the process, you've replaced a dozen middlemen, each wanting a piece of the pie for their expert assistance.

In truth, as in most of life's transactions, you've been on your own all along and just didn't recognize it. The experts are merely cheering you on from the sidelines for a fee.

My own beloved mother, a talented salesperson and an independent woman in many ways, nonetheless relied on experts and outside opinions for many of her decisions in life. I once took her on an island vacation that involved a harrowing tram ride in the pouring rain around narrow mountain roads at high speed. We tourists were swaying in our seats as the rear tires of the open-air bus slipped over the edge of the mountainside at every curve, threatening to catapult us to our death.

Several of us shouted for the driver to slow down. He sang out, "I drive these all the time!" My mother patted my leg and whispered, "He knows what he's doing. Did you see his shirt?" I gave a furtive glance toward the embroidery on the left side of his chest that said *Island Tours*. Even though with our own eyes we could see that our lives were at risk, my mother was relying on a guy in a logo-shirt to be the expert. Obviously, we survived, which only added to her belief that our driver was indeed an expert. It works for people in that way. If you believe an expert knows more than you, then most likely he does. If you believe you are capable of making a housing decision on your own, then most likely you are.

In the fifties and sixties experts were revered. Specialization was happening in every field of business, presumably to get people like you and me the information and advice we needed more quickly. In fact, it just created more bureaucracy and delay. It persists today. Insurance companies require you to see the physician who can't help you in order to be referred to the one who can. Government agencies require banks to put you through mandated loan-modification programs you didn't want in order to allow you to apply for the one you do.

People like Charles Schwab™ taught us that we didn't need the guy in the five-thousand-dollar suit placing our stock order. We could do it ourselves.

UPS® said we didn't have to wait a week for the postal service to deliver. It could happen overnight.

We don't even have to subject ourselves to the cable company's bill; we can stream video and movies over the Internet.

Removing the middleman is a personal statement of empowerment. Instead of the middleman telling you what will happen next in your real estate transaction, you decide what you need or want. Middlemen fight back because a lot of money gets paid to the middle. Auction suggests that you decide how many real estate services you really need and at what cost.

# CHAPTER 14

## THE GREAT AUCTIONEERS MAKE AUCTIONS

Tommy Williams, co-founder of Williams & Williams and former president of the National Auctioneers Association, has sold multi-million-dollar projects across the US for over fifty years—in front of huge crowds, with squads of ring men and millions of dollars at stake. Yet, it's not the size and scope of what he's sold, but his innate ability to handle any situation and turn any auction into a success that makes him legendary. He continues to deliver big economic wins for Williams & Williams' clients, but the smaller ones speak to his caring and character.

On one particular auction day, he phoned the crew to say he was running late to the auction because he was lost. They told him to look up on the hilltop at a big plume of smoke. "The house is on fire and the fire trucks are on the way! Just follow the smoke!"

When Tommy pulled onto the lawn, the crowd of registered bidders stood mesmerized by the house ablaze in front of them. A government agency had seized the home and the representative in charge was beyond upset. Tommy gave her his big reassuring grin and said, "Well, now, it's all going to be just fine. You stand right over here and let's get started." He grabbed the microphone, introduced himself to the crowd, and told them, to the tune of squawking radios and pressurized water, that as they could clearly see, the property on which they'd come to bid was going up in flames right behind him *and* that this was the best news any of them could ever have! They would have had to pay to tear this place down and now someone had done that for them. And what they really wanted—the pad, the plumbing, the infrastructure—was still there and just waiting for them to build the place that was right for them.

"In fact, this entire property has been *improved* and is *more valuable* than it was thirty minutes ago!" Tommy said with such genuine belief in his own words that the crowd smiled back at this charismatic silver-haired fellow and nodded agreement. When he announced it was time to get down to business and trade, they bid wildly for this property and the burned-down home brought *more* than the last list price!

On a very different day, Tommy drove to a small town to auction off a boarded-up nursing home that had belonged to a bank for years.

A defunct nursing home is one of the more difficult properties to sell because, once the doors are closed, it has to go through quite a laborious and expensive process to be recertified and re-opened.

The town couldn't support a nursing home and, apparently, no one living in the town could think of anything else to do with this property, or perhaps they simply didn't have the desire. Tommy pulled up to the site where a stray dog was the only visible life form. A less experienced auctioneer would have phoned the office, said somebody should be hanged for not delivering a crowd, and then driven off.

Tommy knew immediately that no crowd could be drawn for this kind of asset in this kind of town. He walked up and down in front of the property until a man across the street came over to find out what he wanted. Tommy introduced himself to the fellow, whose name was Ben, and told him there was supposed to be an auction today, as evidenced by the signs, but no one had showed up. He asked Ben what he did for a living, how many people lived in the town, and what had happened to the nursing home. In fifteen minutes, Tommy and Ben were good friends.

"Why aren't you interested in this property, since you live across the street?" Tommy inquired. Ben replied that it was a nursing home, then joked that he didn't have any reason to go over there early.

"If you *were* buying it, what would you pay for it?" Tommy asked. "I wouldn't give you more than $25,000 for it," Ben spat.

"Have you ever been inside?" Tommy asked in a tone that put a tour of this facility right up there with a pit pass at the Indy 500.

The man said it was locked up. Tommy asked if he had any bolt cutters to "get that chain off." Ben went back to his house to hunt for weapons of minor destruction.

About this time Tommy spotted another fellow walking down the street, who asked if he'd missed the auction. He said he didn't intend to bid but he'd wanted to watch. Tommy said the auction didn't draw a big crowd, and he introduced himself to the man, whose name was Hiram.

"Just out of curiosity, what would you pay for this place if you *were* buying it?" Tommy asked.

"Nobody wants this place. Been for sale for years. I wouldn't give you $20,000 for it," Hiram said.

About then, Ben arrived with the bolt cutters. Tommy introduced the two men and said, "This fellow Ben lives right across the street. I'm surprised in a town this size you two don't know each other. Anyway, Ben, here, said he wouldn't give over $25,000 for this place, if he were buying. Wouldn't you give $35,000? You seem to know more about it than he does."

"Haven't even been inside." Hiram laughed.

"We can cure that." Tommy snapped the chain with the bolt cutters and led the two men on a tour of a facility he'd never been in.

After the tour, Tommy said, "Now, gentlemen, it's time to get serious. This bank doesn't want to own a nursing home. One of you two is smart enough to figure out something to do with it. I could take a bid of $25,000, but that's just too low to be a serious offer. How about you give me $35,000?"

Hiram paused, then nodded.

"Now, sir," Tommy addressed Ben with his trademark grin, "you could definitely use this. My word, *it's right across the street* from you! Doesn't look to me like you have parking over there where you are, and this would be a great parking lot. How about you give me fifty thousand?"

"Forty-five," Ben said resolutely.

Hiram shook his head, indicating he was out of the bidding.

"Forty-five it is, congratulations. I have a contract for you to sign, and I believe the bank would be crazy not to accept your offer!"

Tommy epitomizes the attributes of a great auctioneer, beginning with the ability to create an auction where there is none. Tommy auditions, selects, trains, and polishes our auctioneers, which to date number thirty auction teams, all of whom share many of the attributes of a great auctioneer.

**The Ability to Read People & Genuinely Connect With Them—** The most talented auctioneers can drive up to the location where the auction is about to take place, scan the crowd, give a subtle nod to one of the ring men, and say, "There's your buyer." The buyer could be leaning up against the picket fencing with a ball cap pulled down over his eyes and look like he wishes he were anywhere but at this auction, yet the auctioneer intuitively knows he wants this house. How he knows, the great auctioneer himself can't explain other than to say, "You're just born with it."

The great auctioneers are nearly psychic when it comes to the day of the sale. They can sense in the crowd if something isn't right—something's not being addressed that should be.

In a matter of seconds, the auctioneer knows when a bidder wants to be the center of attention and acknowledges her, or likes being kidded and jokes with her. When someone wants to participate but is too nervous or afraid, he pauses in the middle of his chant and says, directly to the lady who hasn't moved a muscle, "Ma'am, you look to me like you'd like to bid." And suddenly she does and in fact becomes the winner.

Auctioneers are generally the most people-loving group of individuals you'll ever meet. Everyone they meet is a friend.

**Confidence (not Arrogance)**—Auction is live theater. After the music is written, the orchestra rehearsed, the stage lit, the scenery constructed and painted, the tickets sold, and the marketing people are congratulating themselves on their unparalleled brilliance in delivering a huge crowd, the lead singer, the auctioneer, still has to show up and knock the audience's socks off. A lone auctioneer stands in front of the crowd and sells or doesn't sell that property. That takes a seasoned, confident, talented real estate auctioneer. Just because someone has an auction license or went to auction school or has been in the auction industry for decades doesn't mean they're good at their craft.

**Controlling a Crowd**—There's an art to maintaining control with the right attitude and tone, yet allowing a crowd to question or vent. It's not uncommon when selling a vacant home that someone will try to divert the crowd's attention, shouting something like, "I think everyone should know that I'm the next-door neighbor and the driveway that goes with this house is two feet over on my property." In every case, the person wants attention or to squelch the sale, sometimes because he wants to buy the home himself. The great auctioneer never shuts him down but listens to the information, shares it with the crowd, and then picks up where he left off.

An individual in the crowd might shout, "No one who ever owned this restaurant ever made a go of it, and that's because there's a ghost in the kitchen who throws things!" The auctioneer might say, "Folks, this gentleman right here says this restaurant is up for sale again because there's a ghost in the kitchen. Now I don't know if that's true, but he looks like an honest fellow and he most likely believes what he's telling you. Looks to me like there's nobody in the kitchen right now... and that with a little fixing up, the right owners, and the right plan, this place could become the finest restaurant in town. So if you've ever dreamed of owning one, now is your chance." The auctioneer acknowledged the person in the crowd, didn't try to stifle his story, shared it, and moved on to the business of the day. That takes poise, a way with people, and command of every situation.

Auctions can have distractions, everything from traffic to babies crying. Calling a crowd to order takes just the right touch. If they feel reprimanded, they don't feel like bidding. If they're not convinced to pay attention, they distract from the business of the day.

**Knowing the Value of Real Estate**—If you don't know why this real estate is worth more, then you won't get more. Auctioneers who've sold a great deal of real estate across the country have a pretty good idea of what something will bring in the next thirty days in a particular market. To be a real expert in the field, you must have conducted hundreds of sales. You don't want a surgeon who's performed one successful gall-bladder surgery removing yours unless you're a very trusting soul. And you don't want the fellow who does one real estate auction a year selling your home.

**And of Course the Chant**—Many, myself among them, find the auctioneer's chant mesmerizing as well as entertaining. If you've never attended a live auction you've missed hearing some of the great auctioneers trade. But why do we chant? Many auctioneers don't. They speak normally, saying, "Would you like to bid?" And in fact, an auctioneer who simply asks for bids in a charming accent often leads high-end art auctions.

Chanting is an ancient activity. Primitive people have chanted in every culture around campfires, sacred stones, and unwitting sacrifices since the beginning of mankind.

Perhaps the drafty old cathedrals of the medieval church hold the key. We like to envision an orderly crowd with heads bowed listening to the celebrant at the head of the church; but this was pre-public address systems, closed-circuit TV, Twitter®, or Facebook®, not to mention air-conditioning or heat. Most likely the crowd in the back was chewing on bread and talking to a neighbor. The most expeditious way to keep people focused was to require them to repeat the words of the celebrant. He chants, the congregation echoes his words. We see evidence of that style even now in the Episcopal and Catholic religions.

If you leap to something more frivolous, why do we chant inane phrases at football games...usually about the time our team is braced at the five-yard line trying to keep the opposing team from scoring? The chant is our way of directing all our energy toward a critical moment. The chant demands attention and signals that something crucial is about to happen.

And so the auctioneer reads the terms and conditions of the sale, answers any questions, and then reminds the people that we are about to do business. His chant, centuries old, rings out as a signal that now is the time to focus. Something important is about to take place. In only minutes your real estate will be sold!

**Women Auctioneers**—Auctioneering has been a male occupation for centuries because of its roots. Auction has historically been a family business: the kids set up the merchandise or herded the livestock, mom cooked and clerked, and the girls helped. There was room for only one dominant leader and that of course was dad, who cut the deals and conducted the auctions. When his sons got old enough to contest his position, they generally had to buy him out or go off and start their own auction company. Rigid control was critical in an auction family because if something went wrong at the auction, the family wouldn't get paid and therefore wouldn't eat. It was serious business.

Times have obviously changed and many women have found their place in the industry as auctioneers, usually in the benefit-auction genre or art and antiques, a stereotyping of sorts. The truth is, not all women have voices you can listen to all day long at an auction. High-pitched voices can be grating. (That said, I've heard many a male voice that made me want to rip my hair out.)

I predict the industry will soon see more women selling real estate at auction for the simple reason that women are naturally intuitive and can "read" people, plus they're caring and conscientious.

They know automatically a lot of the things men have to be reminded of. So if a woman is your auctioneer, you should feel good about that...because she's probably had to work harder, and be better than most, to get there.

# CHAPTER 15

## THE DOWNSIDE OF MANAGING THE UPSIDE

Auction is counterintuitive, and often the decisions made about the sale are confusing unless explained.

**WEATHER TOO SEVERE:**

The blizzard's so intense you know no one will show up. We don't cancel the auction. Once we cancelled due to a massive storm in Alaska and immediately received a call from an irate bidder who'd walked a mile in snowshoes to get to the sale site. Bidders will be there. They believe they're the only ones smart enough and strong enough to persevere and make it to the auction, and therefore they'll get the property at a steal. Usually that's the day they have to pay more because everyone had the same idea. Great sales can occur in blizzards, hurricanes, droughts, or any other natural or manmade disaster.

## HOME HAS TO BE FIXED FIRST:

It would seem that fixing your house up makes sense and would bring you more at auction. Amazingly, fixing it up too much may make the buyers nervous that you're going to expect an exorbitant sum and maybe they won't be able to afford it, so they don't attend. Before I ever worked for an auction company, I drove up to the estate sale of a prominent political figure. Attendees were escorted between the various buildings in golf carts, cars were parked in long lines, and traffic cops signaled people where to turn. I made a U-turn and drove away, assuming everyone on the grounds would be bidding and everything would be sold for far more than I could pay.

## CROWD IS TOO SMALL:

Small crowds spell disaster, right? Not necessarily. If they're the right three people you can have a very successful auction. It's all about how much they want it. In fact, we worry more that crowds will be too large, frightening off serious bidders or creating a distraction during crowd control.

## MAKING ATTENDEES VERIFY FUNDS IN ADVANCE:

We held an auction in a nice neighborhood, the home well-kept and not over a year old. People were milling around looking at the yard, the appliances, the closets, all except one man in his late fifties in a ball cap sitting at the marble-topped bar in the living area. He stared at the ceiling, then the fireplace, then the floors.

The auctioneer called for everyone to gather on the front lawn. It was time to do business and find this beautiful home a new owner. The bidding began and, somewhere around two hundred thousand dollars, the man in the ball cap began to bid, nervously and sporadically. Just shy of four hundred thousand dollars, the man in the ball cap became the winner. He began to shake all over and went back inside and sat down at the bar.

Our staff brought him the contract and congratulated him as he sputtered, "My wife is going to kill me. I was on the way to the convenience store and I saw your signs and just thought I'd watch. Then I came in here and realized it was my dream home...everything I'd ever wanted. Then you started the auction and it was too late to call my wife and now I own it." An hour later, his wife appeared, the look on her face clearly saying she had not been consulted. But one look at the house and she flung her arms around her husband, awarding him hero status.

Over half the people who come to a real estate auction aren't certain they're going to attend until the day of the auction. A more stunning fact is that, despite lack of planning, many of them become the high bidder. That's why we keep the barrier to entry low. If everyone has to show up with a certified check, a letter from their bank, or other criteria, many times the potential buyer feels it just takes too much effort since he doesn't know for sure he'll be the winner.

## TRYING TO FILTER THE "RIFF-RAFF":

Sellers often say they don't want people looking at their home who can't afford it. In today's casual society, you can no longer tell who has money and who doesn't simply by the way they dress or behave. The guy who looks like he can't afford his next tank of gas could own the petroleum company. Who has money and who doesn't is best determined by the auctioneer when people are bidding.

## WANTING TO GO TO AUCTION TO "SEE WHAT IT WILL BRING":

If you've managed to talk an auction company into auctioning your home to "see what it will bring," the reserve is inevitably set so high that the property won't sell. You believe the high reserve protected your property when in fact it simply stopped the sale, which is what you wanted to happen because you were just taking the pulse of the market...at the expense of your property.

## SELECTING A COMPANY SOLELY ON COMMISSION RATE:

Auction companies who compete for business solely on commission rates are showing you signs of desperation, and you don't want to be in desperate hands. Will they shave your marketing budget to make their profit? Do they have skilled marketers on staff or have they lost key people to companies who are doing better? Commission cuts are a short-term bargain against a long-term loss. (Commission structures will be discussed in Chapter 21.)

LETTING THE BUYER PICK UP THE TAB:

Many auction companies will tell you that they'll take a reduced commission or perhaps no commission and simply get paid from the buyer's premium (BP), which Williams & Williams® defines as a percentage of the high bid that will be added to the purchase price and paid by the buyer. In some instances auction companies charge the buyer a BP as high as 10-15 percent and the seller gets a "free ride" or pays no commission. But as adults we know nothing's free and you pay in the end. Our experience is simply that once the buyer's premium exceeds what is reasonable or nominal, the buyer simply bids less for the real estate because he or she is taking into account the added-on buyer's premium.

Further, we've watched people nervously trying to calculate the BP and add it to their last bid as the auctioneer is racing to the next bid increment. When bidders get confused, they stop bidding. They become unfocused—no longer competing but only calculating costs. The sale will suffer and the seller has now paid for his free ride in the form of a lower high-bid price.

Buyer's premium is probably one of the hottest-debated topics in the industry. All companies treat it differently for various reasons. In principle, WW believes the buyer should not pay a buyer's premium—the seller should pay the full commission because he will benefit from a buyer whose mind is on ownership, not math. If a buyer's premium is necessary, (which occurs when banks request that auction companies pay former listing brokers, buyer's brokers, and/or outsourcers in addition to their own auction and marketing expenses) then the BP should be kept low enough that the buyer isn't focused on it. We recognize that many genres of real estate are always sold with a BP and therefore it's simply part of doing business.

### LISTING YOUR PROPERTY FIRST TO TRY TO GET MORE:

Once you place a value on your residence or commercial building, you've just told the buyer the upper limits of what it's worth to you. They may feel like an idiot if they pay more than you're asking. Conversely, if you don't put a price on your real estate but merely invite the buyer to compete with others who want it, what it might bring is limited only by the buyer's desire to own it.

Think about yourself when you've hunted for a home. It didn't matter what someone was *asking* for the house you wanted; it was simply what you were willing or able to pay. The high asking price only served to scare you away from some homes versus others.

If you wanted a home enough to make an offer, it was always below the asking price. (Why do they call it "making an offer" or "asking price" versus "the price"?) Because it's not going to be more than the asking price and it's certainly going to be less. So if that's the case, your purchase through the traditional real estate agent method is a downhill negotiation. They have an asking price, you make an offer, and they make a counteroffer. It's a slow, clumsy two-person negotiation that can span days or weeks, and throughout the process you may not even know who's on the other end. Your real estate agent feeds you information: "They're a lovely family and I think they want this house." Or, "They're looking at several and their plane leaves in the morning so I think it's between your house and one other, which is priced more in their range."

Envision how much more exciting and timely an auction is with ten, twenty, thirty, or a hundred people in attendance. For the seller, he sees everything out in the open and doesn't go to bed at night wondering if the buyer will finally sign or merely counter again. For the buyer, he bids readily because he sees the people next to him concurring on the value of this asset. He feels smart for raising his bid, not stupid for countering an offer in the blind.

COUNTERINTUITIVE:
How you've managed your real estate sale in the past may be just the

opposite of the way we'll handle your real estate at auction. So it's important that you select the auction company you trust and then trust the auction company you've selected—and understand the counterintuitive nature of auction. Any attempt to manage the perceived downside of real estate auction inevitably caps your upside.

# CHAPTER 16

## THE LONG ROAD TO SHORT SALES

In a study by Corelogic®, a leading provider of mortgage information, it's noted that "Roughly one in every three homes is mortgage free, according to federal and industry estimates." Home equity is highest in states whose residents tend to be affluent—New York and Hawaii top the list, where about half the population has greater than 50 percent equity in their home. For many, paying off our mortgage has not only become a desire but an obsession.

Nonetheless, a good many homeowners are underwater on their mortgage loan. They're not looking for a payoff but an escape hatch. I want to address selling your home if you're underwater (also known as a short sale) in case you or someone you know is in that situation.

In early 2011, Mitt, a real estate broker, asked us for help. Mitt's wife was ill and trips to Maryland for treatment had used up his funds.

He was losing his home. He'd tried to sell the property but hadn't had any luck. The bank, according to Mitt, wasn't interested in returning his calls.

We contacted Mitt's mortgage servicer and asked if they could tell us what they might accept at short sale. (A short sale is a payoff of the mortgage loan that falls short of the balance owed.) The only dialogue the bank wanted was an offer. They told us we were welcome to market the property and hold the auction at our expense and then bring them a buyer, but they wouldn't agree to any short-sale payoff amount in advance of the auction. They wanted to make sure they got "full value" for their property.

In Mitt's case, full value from our perspective would be a plan to get him out of the house he couldn't afford and allow a family who could afford it to buy his home before it became a vacant and non-earning asset. We took the property to auction and in thirty days obtained a high bid that covered 85 percent of the first mortgage and 76 percent of the first and second mortgages combined. The bank said the offer was indeed attractive but they didn't want to pay our commission, which after fees and marketing would net our company 2 percent. We decided to eat the cost as a learning experience.

Ironically, we are not novices at short sales. ASAP® (Assisted Sale Auction Program), a highly effective B-2-B foreclosure avoidance program created by my business partner Dean Williams, is designed to handle large quantities of short sales, hassle-free, for banks. You would think handling five hundred homes in bank-sanctioned short sales each month would be far more difficult than handling one short sale initiated by a consumer. Oddly just the opposite is true. We learned that going to the large mortgage servicer/banker as a consumer or real estate agent wanting a short sale is akin to surgery without anesthetic.

We conducted the auction, but before the bank could consider the payoff amount we were offering on the first mortgage, they required we talk to the bank holding the second mortgage to see what they were willing to accept. We reminded them that *they* were the bank holding the second mortgage. They acknowledged that but added that the "first department" wasn't allowed to talk to the "second department."

For seven weeks, we talked to the bank and delivered messages back and forth from the second to the first and vice versa, not only determining what they would accept from the troubled borrower but what they would accept internally from each other.

Meanwhile, the buyer, our high bidder at auction, phoned on the forty-ninth day to say, "I'm hanging in here but this is taking a long time and I found this other house. Same neighborhood but it's bigger and this bank has lowered its price. It's $30,000 more, but I can get *this* deal done." We phoned the mortgage servicer, who agreed that they didn't want to lose the buyer, but said that process took precedence over problem solving.

Many mortgage servicers are required to submit short-sale offers through multiple loan-modification programs before the short sale can even be considered by the short-sale department, if there is one. Then the offer may go through another gauntlet of short-sale divisions, none of whom talk to each other.

Our WW people are smart and tenacious, and therefore this story had a happy ending. The bank approved the short sale and the seller was able to breathe again.

You've undoubtedly been reading that the government and mortgage servicers have lots of new programs to get you through a short sale. By the end of 2011, mortgage servicers were offering the troubled homeowner as much as thirty-five thousand dollars to allow the bank to do a short sale. The rules change daily. The caveat is that every program depends on your tenacity.

If you're underwater on your mortgage, you may want to contact your bank to discuss a "workout"—that's an opportunity to stay in the home and lower the monthly payments, or lower the interest rate or get a principal write-down or perhaps even rent to stay. If there's a difference between what you borrowed from your bank and what you get at short sale via auction, can you write a check for the difference? Can you arrange to take out a small loan to repay the difference?

Can you borrow from relatives or friends? Could you bring a partial amount of cash to the table to encourage the bank to take the short sale? Not easy to accomplish if you're already in financial trouble, but possible with some creative thought. And remember, in some states, even though a bank settles with you and forgives full payment of your mortgage, it may legally pursue you for its loss. In addition, the IRS can tax you on the forgiven amount as earned income. (About.com Tax Planning cites information about The Mortgage Forgiveness Debt Relief Act of 2007, which was extended to 2012 by The Emergency Economic Stabilization Act.) And finally, although you may have escaped bankruptcy and not had to pay the bank what you owe, your credit may show a ding for the transaction. You may want an attorney to take a look at any documents you sign releasing you from the mortgage.

*Realtybiznews* quoting *CNN Money* reported that, "In 2010, short sale fraud accounted for more than half the total number of fraud investigations conducted by mortgage lenders like Fannie Mae™ and Freddie Mac™."

The mortgage industry rumbles over short sales being a large source of fraud. For example, a fraudster offers to get the homeowner out of trouble by getting the bank to take a short sale. Let's say the owner owes the bank $200,000. The fraudster goes to the bank with an offer of $125,000, while behind the scenes fraudulent appraisers get the bank comfortable with the lowball offer. Once the bank accepts the offer, the fraudster sells the house to a buyer he has waiting in the wings for $165,000, pocketing a quick $40K. Neither the homeowner nor the bank realizes what's happened.

How can this fraudulent behavior go on without being detected? Because a traditional real estate sale is not open, public, transparent, and competitive.

The right way to handle short sales is to have the auction company and the seller meet with the bank and agree to a payoff "short" of what is owed them. Then the auction company and the seller put together worst-case contingency plans: What if the auction doesn't generate enough to cover the loan balance at the bank? Does the seller bring cash, take out a signature loan for the difference, or have the remaining balance forgiven by the bank? Then the homeowner can go to auction knowing he is prepared for the worst and poised for the best.

In June 2008, the Joint Economic Committee of Congress noted that the average foreclosure cost $77,935, while preventing a foreclosure cost only $3300. Foreclosure costs accounted for 40 percent of the loss on the property at resale. So work with your auction company, or with a real estate agent who specializes in short sales, to accomplish yours. Banks don't like losses and are usually receptive to what you want to accomplish but are often simply process-deficient. That means you have to stay on "TOP" (Thorough, Organized, and Persistent) of the short-sales activity.

**Thorough—find out the rules.** Understand what you have to do to be considered and in what order you have to do it. Keep notes: never hang up from a conversation without noting to whom you spoke, on what day, at what time, and what was decided. Understand if a short sale is allowed. Will they agree in writing not to pursue you for the deficit? What will you have to pay in taxes because the forgiven amount is most likely taxable?

**Organized.** Get all your paperwork together, e.g. loan documents. Know when you ceased paying your mortgage, if you did, and why you did. Prepare a letter of hardship explaining in detail why you found yourself in a circumstance where you couldn't pay and what you did to try to remain current on your mortgage.

**Persistent.** Set up a calendar that reminds you to check with the bank. It's not good enough to hear, "We're working on it." You need to understand what that means, *who* is working on it, and how you can help. You also need to know what's happening to your credit, if anything, while they're working on it and when they'll have an answer for you.

Many times banks or mortgage servicers will require that your application for a short sale, or any other program, be electronic.

Be persistent in checking the status of all activity. Maintain the same kind of notes you would keep if you were talking to a real person. At what time did you enter the information online? Were you able to print something for your records?

If you're short on money, you must be long on patience. It could pay off for you in the end by helping preserve all or part of your credit, getting you out of your old debt problems, allowing you to move on with your life, and giving you a sense of self-worth because you didn't resort to jingle-mail—the sound made by the keys you sent back to the bank.

# CHAPTER 17

## AN OSTRICH THINKS ITS ASS IS COVERED

A rancher who made his money in real estate, when asked how to get rich, said, "People don't get rich knowing when to buy. They get rich knowing when to sell."

The irony is that people buy readily and sell reluctantly. I attribute that to everyone's need to feel smart or, conversely, not look stupid by selling too low or too soon and thereby getting too little. When they're thinking of buying, there's pressing competition. Someone might snatch the deal out from under them. But when they're thinking of selling, the drudgery of listing, showing, and waiting is more depressing than pressing.

Sellers phone our company to say they "made a killing" when they bought a piece of real estate and now they want to sell and cash out. They're implying that the profit is already in the asset and they simply want to access it. All we know is that they own something. We won't know if any financial upside was created as a result of that purchase, until the auction is over.

Markets shift every hour of every day, real estate characteristics alter, features deteriorate, neighborhoods change, and the economy lurches up and down. You bought at a moment in time and you will sell at a moment in time. "The buy" merely put you in the game. "The sell" determines the score.

This is where the ostrich behavior begins, although to be entirely accurate, an ostrich doesn't bury his head in the sand. That's a myth. According to the American Ostrich Association, the mere existence of which proves there's an organization for everything, "the male ostrich will dig a large hole (up to 6 to 8 feet wide and 2 to 3 feet deep) in the sand for the nest/eggs. Predators cannot see the eggs across the countryside, which gives the nest a bit of protection. The hen as well as the rooster takes turns sitting on the eggs and, because of the indention in the ground, usually just blend into the horizon. All birds turn their eggs (with their beak) several times a day during the incubation period. From a distance it appears as though the bird has his/her head in the sand."

I think it's fair to say, that from a distance it can appear that many homeowners sitting on their nest seem to have their head in the sand, simply hoping danger won't arrive and destroy everything they're sitting on.

I've been guilty of that myself in holding on to assets too long—the home I described and also with overexposure in the stock market: watching my investments slide to eighty cents on the dollar but holding on, certain it was just a market blip. Blinking hard as my portfolio took a dip to seventy cents on the dollar but encouraged by experts who swore it would recover. Then another plunge to fifty cents on the dollar and I told myself it was too late now; I couldn't possibly sell at this point, I had to ride it out. At twenty cents on the dollar, nearly catatonic over my loss, I felt like a certifiable fool for not taking seventy or even fifty. I laid low and watched it go. Why couldn't I sell?

It's the front end (the buy) that helps us create the "number in our head." If a property was listed for $580K for three years and you bought it for $300K, within twenty-four hours of signing the closing documents, you believe you're "in the money"—that if you sold it tomorrow you'd net $280K! Think of the humor in that! During the negotiation, you told yourself it wasn't worth $580K, in fact not a penny over $300K. But the moment you own it, you decide you made a once-in-a-lifetime buy and it really *is* worth $580K.

Our ego wants us to believe that purchasing at $300K was a result of our shrewd business sense, our ability to spot a diamond in the rough, our innate talent in persuading and trading better than any other buyer. We never believe the seller suddenly realized the number in *his* head wasn't reality and simply gave in to current market value. Of course not, he surrendered to our superior negotiating techniques.

The dialogue going on in the seller's head is equally flawed. "If my first real estate agent had done his job, this would have sold for $580K while the market was hot, but he dinked around and cost me money." "It's worth every bit of $580K, but I'm tired of fooling with it and I'm going to get it off my back." Rather than, "Current market value proved my number to be an aspiration, not a reality."

**Three rules for an "ostrich":**

1. Laying low (sitting on your nest) is the same thing as doing nothing to change your situation. And you have a "situation" or you wouldn't be laying low.

2. If your current situation is likely to get dramatically worse, laying low (hoping something will hatch) could put you in more danger.

3. If your decision about your situation is based on fear—"If I sell now I'll lose my upside" or "If I sell now I've already *lost* my upside"—then you're in analysis paralysis and have lost focus on what you could do, be,

have, or accomplish with the money you still have. What could you do right now with the present return on your investment, whatever that is? Think about it, and then do *that*.

In Chapter Eleven, I mentioned auctioning my city home. I carefully "managed" the value of my home knowing I would never let it go for seventy cents on the dollar. The first appraisal came in at roughly $450,000. Clearly insane! I had paid $420K when I bought the place and I'd put another $150K into the remodeling. Obviously this appraiser knew nothing and I needed to find a smarter one. I went down the list to another appraiser, who I felt would understand my neighborhood better than the first. The second appraisal came in at roughly $625,000.

Now that was more like it, I thought. "This fellow gets it…but obviously not completely. He doesn't realize the value of all the repairs and work I've put into the house so I'm going to bump that value just a little and I can always come down to his appraised value when I negotiate with a buyer. My list price on my house? $720,000.

My life became all about selling the house for that number, and my real estate agent just didn't get it. Therefore I let her six-month listing agreement run out and happily took over the sale myself. Listed "For Sale By Owner"…twelve months.

Prior to taking over the marketing myself, I was mad at the real estate agent. Now I was just mad at the general public. What was wrong with these people? They wandered up and knocked on my door at all hours, sauntered through my weekly open houses, some even measured and chatted, and then no offers. One man came in and offered me $460,000 and I "showed him the door."

Time is money and carrying costs mark the months for sellers like me: roughly $6000 per month for both mortgages plus property taxes and $1000 a month to mow, repair, winterize, trim trees, and keep the landscaping groomed.

I moved out in month thirteen, so the home was vacant for another year. But I drove forty-four miles round trip, three times a week, to check on the house: were there leaks due to the rainstorm, was the window caulking chipping off, was the yard work being done, did the plumbing still work? Not to mention the times the burglar alarm went off in the middle of the night and I had to race into town to meet the police.

How much does a vacant asset depreciate? (As much as 2 percent per month, according to many mortgage servicers, who should know since they have a lot of depreciating assets.) It also costs an incredible amount of peace of mind. In fact, a vacant unoccupied home's depreciation should be measured in human-hair loss, gum recession, insomnia, and nail-biting.

Seven hundred and thirty days of showings, phone calls, and open houses later, my home sold at auction for $467,000, despite the fact that I'd worn it out by showing it to everyone breathing, rejecting offers, and basically giving the home a bad reputation. (To put this value in perspective, a $467K home in Tulsa today is equivalent to a 1.5-1.8 million dollar home in New York or LA.)

Had I sold the home at auction on day one, I would have saved twenty-four months of mortgage payments and upkeep and twelve months of depreciation. I spent $309,492, or 43 percent of my home's perceived value, holding on.

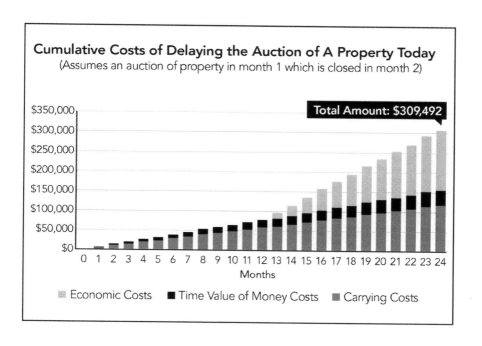

Even if I had been able to find a buyer for $720K, I would not have netted $720K. The real net on the sale of my house at $720K after two years of holding costs would have looked like this:

| | Sell Month 24 | |
|---|---|---|
| Starting List Price[1] | $720,000 | |
| Economic Cost of Holding the Property[2] | - $151,200 | |
| | $568,800 | *Subtotal* |
| Carrying Cost of Holding the Property[3] | - $120,000 | |
| | $448,800 | *Subtotal* |
| Time Value of Money Cost of Holding the Property[4] | - $38,292 | |
| **Actual List Price** | **$410,508** | *Total* |
| **Sale Price at Auction[5]** | **$467,000** | *Total* |

**Footnotes:**
1. List price of property.
2. Deprecation and/or deterioration, market deterioration, and overexposure to the market (1.75% a month for 12 months while the property was vacant).
3. Mortgage Interest = $4K per month and Upkeep/Maintenance = $1K per month for 24 months.
4. Difference between the Net Present Value (NPV) of $720,000 in 2 months and the NPV of $720,000 in 24 months, using an annual discount rate of 3%.
5. The sale price at auction after 24 months of trying to sell the property.

According to Investopedia, "NPV compares the value of a dollar today to the value of that same dollar in the future, taking inflation and returns into account." Simply put, money tomorrow isn't the same as money right now. Dollars "depreciate" in value. If you don't believe that, try to buy a loaf of bread with the same money you could buy it with three years ago.

## Here's my pain in a pie chart:

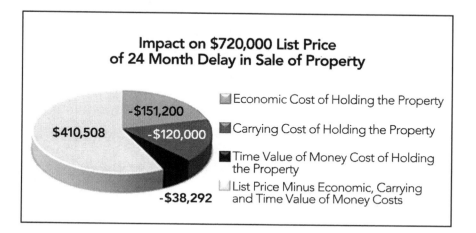

**Impact on $720,000 List Price
of 24 Month Delay in Sale of Property**

- Economic Cost of Holding the Property
- Carrying Cost of Holding the Property
- Time Value of Money Cost of Holding the Property
- List Price Minus Economic, Carrying and Time Value of Money Costs

$410,508
-$151,200
-$120,000
-$38,292

## My real estate experience proved:

1. My $720K list price was a number in my head—it wasn't current market value, even on day one.

2. Had I accepted any offer above $410K early on, I would have saved an enormous amount of cash, time, and anxiety, and I would have come out ahead financially.

3. I got $467K at auction in month 25. Imagine how much more I would have gotten if I'd auctioned in month one...something close to last list.

That's why I go crazy when I see other sellers making the same mistake.

A fellow I know has had his long-vacant home on the market for over four years. It sits on several untended acres. People in this part of the country who've tried to buy it say, "He's real proud of it," meaning his asking price is too high. I've talked to him about selling at auction but he just can't do it. He's hanging on to that number in his head because he put in a gourmet kitchen and he knows that kitchen is what makes the house worth 200 percent more than anyone has offered him in four years of marketing and showing the place. That kitchen has cost him a lot. And when it comes to selling his house, believe me, nothing's cooking.

# CHAPTER 18

## WEIGHING THE PRICE OF PERSONAL FREEDOM

"I'm not going to give it away!" you shout about the time we discuss the reserve price for your home. (The price below which you do not have to sell it.)

There's a law of physics that says energy is neither created nor destroyed but only transformed. The same is true with the concept of "giving away" anything. There is no circumstance in which you give something away that you do not receive a counter-balancing measure of something in return.

At the most tangible level, if I give a home away to charity, I'm a generous human being, but I also get something in return—a tax write-off. If I give the little house down the street to my son and his wife, I get something in return—having my grandchildren near me. We always get something in return because that's how the universe balances energy, even if the something we get is a life's lesson or an understanding of business or the joy of giving.

Auction gives nothing away. Something comes back in return— cash! What if it's not enough cash to satisfy my needs, you ask? Then you have to weigh the price of your personal freedom. If you're selling a house as part of a divorce, you're freeing yourself of bad memories. If you're selling your home because you've already bought another, then you're freeing yourself from endless trips to care for the old place and endless bills to maintain it while it sits empty and deteriorating. Auction is freedom. How much is freedom worth? If the number in your head, the one you can't seem to turn into a check for that amount, is more important than freedom, you may need to stay chained to your real estate a while longer.

If you have a home you absolutely love and never want to leave it, I applaud you. I feel exactly that way about my ranch. But here are a few statements I hear repeatedly from people who call to talk about selling their home.

"I hate this place but I can never sell it because I wouldn't get anything for it." (And since you "hate it" what are you getting from it now?)

"This place is like a tomb now that my husband's gone, but he always loved it and never wanted me to sell it." (But he's not there to bump around late at night in the loneliness, is he?)

"I'm not going to sell it because I'd have to give her half the money!"

(As they say on *Saturday Night Live*, "Really? Spite is holding you back? Really??")

Freedom comes in many guises—mental, emotional, and physical. The price of freedom has nothing to do with whether auction brings you more than last list or below what you expected. Selling at auction frees you for what's new and what's next—without torturing you for a year or two in the process.

We conducted an auction for a wonderful artist who, due to health issues, wanted to return home to Europe. Time was critical and money was necessary. He could not allocate funds upfront for marketing. He also could not have a failed auction—he simply didn't have time.

Like all sellers, he had a number in his head, and when it came to his property, he didn't want to "give it away." After many conversations with him, we agreed to underwrite the auction of his home with "an assured purchase price," meaning if we failed to achieve a particular minimum value then we would make up the difference or buy the home for that amount. This put the deliverable squarely on our shoulders because it was our money entirely at risk. The downside, if it occurred, was all ours and the seller was protected. The upside was good for both of us.

The sale was complicated by the resort community's dislike of auction and their very strict rules regarding advertising. They didn't allow classified ads, signs in the yard, open houses, or the option to advertise or hold the auction at the closest hotel. No events of any kind.

After some research, we held the auction twenty miles from the home in a nice hotel and broadcast it live on Auction Network® to everyone logged in remotely. The home sold for more than 200 percent of the reserve.

There wasn't a dry eye in the house—everyone ecstatic for the seller who had become our client and, as so often is the case when you know their stories, our friend as well.

The sale is only half of the transaction. The closing is the other half. The stock market plummeted, and the buyer's funding fell through. The seller left for Europe, no longer the owner of the home, having exercised his right to have us purchase the home at the agreed-upon minimum.

Think of your own situation. Make a mental list of all the things you could own, do, experience, or become if you were not tied to a home you no longer want or need. If all of those things could be realized with the auction of your real estate, then I recommend you trade "wait and worry" for personal freedom. It's the best real estate decision you'll ever make.

# Chapter 19

## Nine Basic Auction Methods

The auction company has to determine the type of auction that's best for your property. Below are a few auction types and techniques.

1. **Absolute Auctions or Sells Without Reserve:** Many people won't attend an auction unless they know the property is selling Absolute. Life is packed with too many opportunities and responsibilities. They have to pick and choose. If it's a sunny day, do they go to the auction or play golf or ride their dirt bike or clean out their garage? They may not know which will appeal to them until they wake up that morning. Furthermore, if they believe that even though they might be the high

bidder, they'll have to wait perhaps weeks for the seller to approve their high bid, they're less likely to show up.

Why go to open houses, call their bank to arrange a loan, run some numbers on their personal financial situation, and give up their time to attend and bid on the off-chance everything will go well? Thankfully, many people do just that, but they would rather know that if they're the high bidder they will absolutely be the new owner regardless of price. Absolute auctions engender confidence in bidders, and therefore they compete more strongly.

*Consider selling your home at Absolute auction if:*

- You have no mortgage or liens on your property.
- You have mortgages or liens and can verify that you have funds to cover them without using proceeds from the auction.
- You have other property you could have the auction company sell.
- You do not want to front any marketing money.
- You are not in bankruptcy or foreclosure.
- You agree that buyers compete eagerly if they know the high bidder will definitely own the home today.

- You believe in current market value, want to take control and move on with your life.

2. **Sells Without Reserve <u>Above A Certain Dollar Amount</u>:** Once a particular dollar amount is reached at the auction, the property will be sold to the highest bidder. "Sells Without Reserve Above X dollars" gives the buyer confidence that the seller does intend to let go of the property today above a certain value. This only works if the value is obviously reasonable to any potential buyer. For example, a city is selling a facility and, due to many government rules, can't sell the property for under a million dollars. All due diligence indicates the property is worth at least three to five million. Saying that it will sell without reserve above a million dollars is most likely reasonable.

*Consider selling your home without reserve above a certain dollar value if:*
- You have no mortgage or liens on your property.
- You have mortgages or liens and can verify that you have funds to cover them without using proceeds from the auction.
- You would like some of the advantages of an

Absolute sale and the ability to reject the high bid if it fell below a very nominal reserve.

3. **Sells Subject To Seller Confirmation:** This is a reserve auction and it is most banks' way of selling. Nervous about the investors to whom they often have to answer, and any unplanned write-down below the UPB (unpaid balance,) the banks usually have an unannounced reserve. When companies like ours sell these bank assets, we are required to tell the high bidder that they will have to wait for bank approval. The banks give us target values, which may or may not be in line with current market value. Banks may accept high bids that are below these values if the auction company makes a compelling case regarding market conditions. The bad news is that buyers become distrustful of the process as they wait for bank approval, particularly if it's withheld.

For the very same reasons, buyers become irritated with individual sellers who want to confirm/approve the high bid at auction. A good auction company will make sure that the seller places a reasonable reserve so, in effect, the buyer is not impacted by the reserve because approval/confirmation is virtually automatic.

*Consider selling your property with reserve if:*

- You and your auction company are 90 percent confident you can hit that number at auction.

- You have a mortgage or liens on the property that you must pay off with the auction proceeds.

- You're able to front marketing money.

4. **Published Reserve Auctions:** Some auction companies open the bidding at the reserve price. In general, our company doesn't like this practice. The seller who is dead set on his reserve value will often change his mind after the auction if he sees lots of bidding and an auctioneer working to achieve the reserve yet the crowd is unwilling to bid any higher. The seller knows he's witnessed current market value and the majority of the time will approve the high bid. So publishing the reserve is a mental barrier to buyers and thwarts the excitement of auction.

5. **Sealed Bid:** In this type of auction, bidders meet all the criteria for bidding, including any required bid deposit, and submit their highest and best offer in a sealed envelope. On a given day and hour the envelopes are opened and the winner announced. Sealed bid gives

buyers only one swing of the bat and doesn't allow for on-going competition.

6.  **Rolling Sealed Bid With Final Outcry:** This is WW's proprietary variation of a sealed-bid auction. Bids are opened as they arrive by a designated attorney. None of the bidders are told if they're the high bidder, or how much anyone else has bid. They are only notified if they need to increase their bid to remain in the top three and be eligible to attend final outcry, meaning in this case a live auction among finalists.

    Like all sealed-bid auctions, this maintains the anonymity of the bidders, many of whom may not want their names in the paper in high-profile bidding wars, and it keeps the focus on the property, not the potential buyer. However, the added benefit is that it affords bidders more than one chance to compete.

7.  **Dutch Auctions (Reverse Auctions):** These auctions start with a very high number and drop lower and lower. The first person to bid automatically wins. While it creates tension, the bidding is going in the wrong direction. Our auction company wants bidders to have one more chance to bid higher than the next person, which isn't theoretically possible in a Dutch auction.

8. **Multi Par Real Estate Auctions:** Multi Par auctions involve successive rounds of bidding that combine and recombine parcels or tracts of land into different subsets to obtain the most money for the entirety. Recombining and rebidding can go on all day long, and in the end, someone can swoop in and bid on the entirety (all parcels) and win the bid. There are auction companies who utilize this method routinely and successfully. Williams & Williams® prefers Buyer's Choice Absolute.

9. **Buyer's Choice Absolute:** In this method of auction, bidders are competing for "the right to choose first" from a pool of similar properties. For example, houses on the same block, condos, vacant lots, parceled acreage. The high bidder may choose one, some, or all of the "like properties" offered, multiplied by the high-bid amount. If the high bidder takes less than all the properties, then the bidding begins again and the subsequent high bidder now wins the right to choose first.

This method of bidding forces competition across buyer types. If an eighty-acre field, twenty-acre building site, and five acres with a lake cabin are all going to be auctioned today and I want only the lake cabin,

I will not bid until you tell me that you're now going to sell the lake cabin. If, however, you tell me that all three are being sold "buyer's choice" and I must bid to win the right to choose first, then you have forced me to compete with people I would not have to compete with otherwise. Buyer's Choice Absolute increases competition and high-bid values and comes with the absolute assurance that the properties chosen by the high bidders will change hands.

10. **Assured Sales Price:** This is not an auction type but an underwriting of the auction outcome. WW and the seller agree on a sales price, and if the auction company fails to obtain a high bidder at that number the auction company must make up the difference or buy the home for that sum. If the seller chooses to "stay in the deal" until the auction company has re-auctioned the property, then the seller may additionally share in the subsequent profits from the third-party sale.

*Consider an assured sales price if:*

- You own a home in a higher-dollar price range.
- You have no mortgage or a great deal of equity in the home.

- You have a mortgage or liens and can verify that you have the ability to pay them off without proceeds from the real estate auction.

- You want a sum of cash today that is certain, and you like the idea of the chance of additional cash if the home brings even more than expected in a subsequent sale.

- You have issues and opportunities in your life that are more important than the process of selling your home.

Familiarize yourself with the various methods of auction and understand why your auction company has selected one and what they believe it will do for your property. Auction has become a sophisticated business. It spans the Iowa cornfields to Wall Street boardrooms. View your auction company as a partner in solving real estate issues and maximizing real estate opportunities.

# Chapter 20

## How It Works Step by Step

When money's tight and the economy is bad, a lot of people sideline their plans to buy a vacation home and decide to downsize their primary residence in a hunker-down mode. However, a whole lot of other people cash out their 401Ks and say, "To hell with it. I'm buying that lake place I always wanted because I'm making no real return on this glorified savings account!"

In tough times, some people turn totally utilitarian and invest in a laundry business that specializes in washing hospital towels because that need will always exist. Other people purchase a beautifully appointed bed-and-breakfast in the middle of nowhere because, if the world comes to an end, they'd rather share a morning muffin with strangers than worry about hospital laundry.

Real estate is always a great investment if you buy at the right price and sell at the right time. And it's not what type of real estate you invest in that counts, but how you feel about the real estate in which you've invested.

Whether buying or selling, do it through a reputable auction company and understand how they work. Below is a brief synopsis of buyers, sellers, and the auction company's responsibilities and timeline.

### WILLIAMS & WILLIAMS AUCTION COMPANY PROCESS:

An auction listing agreement is prepared for your signature. The property or properties are listed with Williams & Williams® and put on our own Williams & Williams®, WWM Exchange™, and Auction Network® Web sites where applicable. Currently more than 350,000 real estate investors and buyers come to our sites every month, and over 60 percent of them are first-time visitors.

1. Auction Operations sets the auction date and schedules the open houses with seller approval.

2. The condition of your property is assessed, and interior and exterior photos are taken for marketing purposes.

3. Closing begins title work in preparation for the closing.

4. Marketing develops a marketing plan and launches phase I (Web site, story development, and campaign

design around target market-segmentation analytics—matching potential buyers to your home).

5. Buyer calls and inquiries are fielded.

6. Client Services reviews and resolves any disclosure or access issues.

7. Marketing's phase II launches (sign placement, direct mail, virtual tours).

8. Open houses are conducted.

9. Initial marketing results measured.

10. Marketing phase III (Internet keyword, banner ads, e-mail blasts, postcards, print ads, video on Auction Network®, and radio and television launched).

11. Auction Day—property is auctioned and contract signed.

12. Closing group calls high bidder to begin working with buyer to close.

13. Quick Close™ in a few days or close in the traditional thirty days.

## BUYERS' PROCESS—GETTING READY TO ATTEND THE AUCTION:

1. Buyers see the advertising and learn about the auction. This is the time period for questions, answers, and public inspections. They decide how they will make the down payment if they are the successful high bidder.

2.   They log on to www.williamsauction.com or www.auctionnetwork.com to research the property in detail and understand the auction process.

3.   Contact Customer Service to get all information needed.

4.   Attend an open house.

5.   Arrange their finances.

6.   Attend the live auction on site or register on Auction Network® to bid remotely in real time. (Proof of funds and/or a deposit may be required from Auction Network® bidders.)

7.   Register roughly thirty minutes prior to auction with a valid driver's license or proof of ID. There is no fee to register, and for most auctions high bidders may make their down payment in cash or personal check. If bidding remotely through www.auctionnetwork.com, log in thirty minutes in advance to complete registration and get ready to bid.

8.   Auctioneer reads the terms and conditions and answers questions from the crowd.

9.   Once the auction begins, bidders may turn in their bids

by raising their hands, and a ring man or the auctioneer will acknowledge their bid. (Remember that no one ever buys a property by inadvertently scratching his or her nose.)

10. The auctioneer will say "high bidder" if they're the winner. Usually this means they're the winner subject to the seller accepting the high bid (as is the case with bank-owned properties). Other times, the auctioneer will say "sold," meaning the asset is indeed theirs on this day.

11. Once they're the high bidder, they execute a contract on site within minutes of the auction's conclusion, or they sign an electronic contract if they're an Auction Network® bidder.

12. Buyer receives a congratulatory call from Customer Service.

13. Closing, Client Services, and an auction representative work with the buyer to help him through any closing issues.

14. Quick Close™ in just a few days or close in the traditional thirty days.

**THE SELLER'S PROCESS:**

1. List your property with the auction company.

2. Determine if you will offer the buyer Quick Close™ by paying buyer's portion of the closing costs.

3. You're advised of any property issues: title issues, liens you forgot about, property conditions the auction company wants to disclose at sale.

4. You receive updates on the marketing results, open-house attendees, Web hits, and other performance metrics.

5. You are either present at the auction or are informed of the sales results after the auction. You approve the sale according to the terms of your agreement with the auction company.

6. You execute the sales agreement and finally execute any closing documents.

7. Quick Close™ in a few days or close in the traditional thirty days.

8. You receive the funds from the sale of the asset, minus closing costs, the auction company's commission, or other fees as determined by your contract.

**All together, working in concert, it looks like this:**

# 30-Day, Residential Auction Timeline

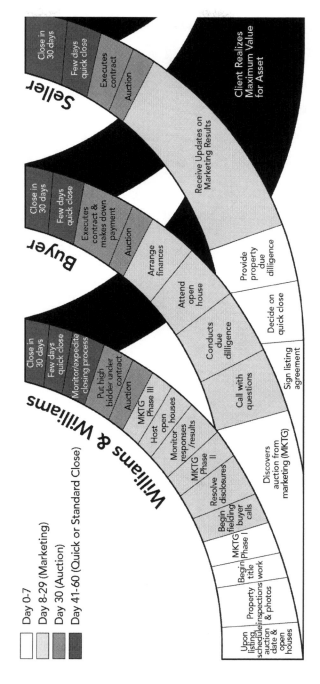

Day 0-7
Day 8-29 (Marketing)
Day 30 (Auction)
Day 41-60 (Quick or Standard Close)

**Williams & Williams**

Upon listing, schedule auction date & open houses
Property inspections & photos
Begin title work
Begin MKTG Phase I
Begin fielding/buyer calls
Resolve disclosures
MKTG Phase II
Monitor responses/results
Host open houses
MKTG Phase III
Auction
Put high bidder under contract
Monitor/expedite closing process
Few days quick close
Close in 30 days

**Buyer**

Discovers auction from marketing (MKTG)
Call with questions
Conducts due dilligence
Attend open house
Arrange finances
Auction
Executes contract & makes down payment
Few days quick close
Close in 30 days

**Seller**

Sign listing agreement
Decide on quick close
Provide property due dilligence
Receive Updates on Marketing Results
Auction
Executes contract
Few days quick close
Close in 30 days

Client Realizes Maximum Value for Asset

For everything to go smoothly, the auction company must execute each task with precision. Rarely does someone outside the auction company understand how important it is to hit the mark right on time.

Occasionally, someone will ask why we don't simply extend the marketing beyond thirty days so people can take their time in performing the various tasks. After decades of managing auctions, we know that there's an urgency window—too long and people procrastinate and lose interest, too short and they don't have time to prepare for the sale. Our timelines are carefully designed to maintain momentum and interest. Like everything else in the auction business, timing is an art.

# CHAPTER 21

## SO WHAT DOES IT COST?

How much do auction companies charge to auction properties? The answer is how much risk do you want the auction company to assume?

If you're a motion-picture stunt man, you have a "day rate" for leaping off buildings and engaging in knife fights. But let's say the studio asks you to attempt a stunt that ended in a funeral for the last two brave souls who tried it. If you accept the gig, your risk just escalated and, most likely, so did your day rate.

Assume you sit down with an investment broker and tell her that you want a 25 percent annual return on your portfolio or you're firing her. She says she can put you into aggressive, high-growth stocks that could bring a 25 percent ROI, but she warns you that the companies aren't proven and therefore the risk to you is substantial if you choose this route. Alternatively, she offers to buy, on your behalf, solid blue-chip stocks, but the return might be 4 percent over several years. Your choice is risk versus return.

From the seller's viewpoint, the primary negotiation between you and the auction company seems to involve commission, reserve, and fronting marketing money and/or turn-down fee, but there's more to it. You and the auction company are engaged in an important psychological exercise to determine how convinced the auction company is that they can successfully sell your property and how seriously committed you are to letting it go.

Sellers will always tell the auction company that they're not only ready to sell but they *have* to sell, and *nothing* would keep them from selling. In fact, many things can make that untrue: they forgot they had a lien on the house from an unpaid contractor, they had no idea their wife would get an attorney and an injunction, they had no idea they'd simply have a change of heart. Auction companies understand that the good intention is there, but good auction companies rely on signed documents that spell out the deal.

RESERVE PRICE & UPFRONT MARKETING MONEY:
If the auction company is risking their money (meaning you're not fronting any marketing money), then the auction company's chance

of recouping that money is dependent on whether or not you accept the high bid at auction and the property closes.

When the reserve price is higher than the property is likely to bring at auction, the auction company has no chance of recovering any cash outlay for marketing or auction expenses, and risks their reputation from a failed sale.

Let's say you have a house that's been on the market for 417 days and was listed at $1.7 million on day one, lowered to $1.5 million six months later, and then to $1.2 million at the one-year mark. You've rejected three offers, all under $700K.

Let's assume you tell the auction company that you will not accept less than $990K for the house and you refuse to front any marketing money, meaning the auction company would have to advance those funds to conduct a sale. The downward spiral is that they won't achieve your reserve, you will reject the high bid, and they will eat their costs and suffer reputational loss. The auction company is in a risk/risk position with no reward.

The auction company might instead offer to sell your property Absolute, meaning they will bring the marketplace and conduct a professional sale, and the high bidder automatically gets the real estate regardless of price. Now the auction company is happy to front all the marketing costs because there is a guaranteed sale and closing.

If you refuse to sell Absolute, then the issue is how much risk the auction company and you are individually willing to take in order to obtain a reward. Each time you lower your reserve, there's less risk for the auction company. The lower the reserve, the less marketing money you're asked to front since the marketing money is calculated as a percent of the reserve. If there is no reserve, meaning it's an Absolute auction, then there's no upfront money.

COMMISSION STRUCTURE:

Some auction companies will sell your real estate for a hundred thousand dollars and charge you only three percent. When a better auction company comes along and says they charge eight percent, you may decide that you would never hire a company at eight percent when you could hire another company for three. So while you paid the novice auction company a commission of $3000 on a hundred-thousand-dollar sale and you netted ninety-seven thousand dollars, it doesn't take a math major to conclude that if you went with the better company at eight percent and they sold the same property for $250K, you'd have a better return on investment.

While you paid the seasoned auction company $20K commission instead of $3K, you gained $150K in the high bid and netted $230K versus $97K. You spent $17K more in commission to net $133K more. I think you'd take that deal all day long!

| | COMPANY A | | COMPANY B |
|---|---|---|---|
| **HIGH BID** | $100,000 | | $250,000 |
| **COMMISSION** | 3%=$3000 | (diff: $17K) | 8%=$20,000 |
| **NET TO SELLER** | $97,000 | (diff: $133K) | $230,000 |

Focusing solely on commission ignores experience and talent. Auction is high-velocity business. Auction companies have to create heat and deliver current market value in record time. That takes expertise *and money*. Oddly, sellers often think the shorter time frame means auction commissions should be lower. In fact, auction companies have to do more and spend more because they only have thirty days to deliver a buyer.

Cut-rate auction companies don't "do it for less"; they simply "do less." They hire less-talented auction staff, spend less on marketing your property, and simply pray someone will show up and bid high—which is like skimping on helium at a balloon festival and hoping the wind picks up.

# CHAPTER 22

## THE GREATEST OFFER IN THE WORLD

Right after the auction marketing breaks, the seller's phone rings off the hook with calls from every fence-straddler in the county. They've just heard that the property is going to auction and that would be a shame. In fact, they want to buy the property right now!

We listed a four-hundred-acre resort that once belonged to a Grammy™ Award-winning celebrity. The log cabins were Ralph Laurenesque, and the grounds were manicured and exquisite in every detail. The sellers didn't want to sell but they were moving away. Nonetheless, the property had been on the market for well over a year, and everyone in a tri-state area had seen it or asked their broker to take a look for them. There were talks of contracts, phone calls to negotiate price, and an all-out determination to "wait out" the seller.

The auction listing agreement was signed and the marketing began.

Within days, the seller's phone began ringing. First his former listing agent called to ask if he could get out of "this auction deal" because he had a buyer. Then came a call from a buyer who said he had a friend who was ready to sign a contract tonight, paying the seller full price, but the buyer was firm that unless he knew for sure the auction was being called off, he wouldn't come forward. Then the "greatest offer in the world," from someone who claimed to be "standing in the middle of the resort property right now with a buyer who has the full price in cash in his briefcase" and just needed the seller to drive out there with a contract! Tempting?

Auctioneers smile because we know we've done our job pulling people off the bench and suiting them up for a game they never intended to play. Where were these buyers twenty-four hours before the marketing broke that announced AUCTION in only thirty days? They were sitting on their fists rocked back on their thumbs...unidentifiable and unmotivated. What set their collective derrieres on fire? Not the real estate sign but the auction sign—the terrifying words that mean get serious or step aside.

Then why not use auction as bait and just sell a property pre-auction? Many B-2-B clients require that approach. Overused, it turns the auction process into a sham. You can't cry wolf and have auction work effectively. Auction only works if it's authentic...if you mean it and believe in it and do it.

Unless it's a bank-owned property, we tell potential buyers to simply bring a signed contract with 10 percent down and give us an acceptance deadline of twenty-four hours after the auction. Alternatively, we will enter the offer as a proxy bid during the auction, and if no one bids higher than that amount, then they will get the house. Obviously, we think their interests are better served by showing up at the auction like everyone else and simply bidding the amount they're willing to pay. Roughly one in five hundred times does the breathless buyer ever arrive in our office with a contract and cash down. They want the auction cancelled because they want time to negotiate with the seller. They aren't serious and auction forces them to get serious.

Buyers who try to scare the seller by saying if the auction goes forward they won't bring an offer and they won't show up, weren't real buyers to begin with. Think about it. If you desperately wanted a particular house, would you refuse to bring a contract or alternatively come and bid? They want the auction called off because auction brings heat and they want the heat turned down. If they can get the auction cancelled, then they have time to get inspectors, stroll through with appraisers, and begin the slow, painful downward price negotiation. "I would have agreed with your asking price, but now that we've looked at the furnace and the roof, it's just not worth that much." You'll never hear that at an auction. Remember, listings go down, bidding goes up.

At a recent auction for a large estate, we received the standard call: "I have the greatest offer in the world…a cash buyer in hand for a million dollars, but they won't sign the contract unless you cancel the auction because they're not going to compete." We said we wouldn't cancel the auction but would love to have the signed offer for that amount. The irritated potential buyer called our seller to say he'd just blown a one-million-dollar cash-in-hand sale by listening to his crazy auction company.

The morning of the sale, our seller confided that he hadn't slept well because he was so apprehensive. His mood brightened as cars started rolling in and a large crowd gathered. In less than a half hour, it was clear it was going to be a huge event. We successfully auctioned the property and the seller was effusive about our people, processes, the auctioneer, and the entire experience. He ended by saying, "My only regret is I didn't do this a year ago." The high bid? Four million dollars. Four times better than the "greatest offer in the world."

# CHAPTER 23

## EFFECTIVE OR DEFECTIVE: ELECTRONIC AUCTIONS

Auction at your fingertips is an electrifying concept. It's thrilling to be able to buy a home at a live auction from the comfort of your couch six states away. Or conversely be able to sit in your offices and watch thirty of your surplus real estate holdings be sold live on the lawn in twelve different states in a single day. Technology has made virtual attendance possible. And it's allowed us to leverage the presence of the great auctioneers across more states in a single day than they could ever reach by plane, changing our real estate selling and purchasing capabilities forever.

For decades, auctioneers believed no one would buy a property unless they could stand on the lawn and see it. After all, it's going to be your home or business, an emotional purchase, and the buyer will want to walk through it and imagine all the things she can do to make it hers.

He or she would certainly not buy a home they hadn't been inside, and if they violated those two premises, then they would definitely not buy a property over fifty thousand dollars via remote technology.

We of course now know that isn't entirely true. Buyers attend an open house in person but often end up bidding from a city or a state away. They find comfort in dozens of photos and uploaded virtual tours and don't require a final walk-through before purchase. Investors buy the less-expensive houses, but families more often than not buy the higher-end homes.

Today, Auction Network® has sold homes ranging from one hundred thousand to two million dollars. Since we launched Auction Network® in 2007, our live interactive bidding community has grown substantially. Hourly, people log in to watch or bid on each individual asset across the US. Visitors from two hundred countries and territories, the top entries in the month of October 2011, were the US, China, Canada, South Korea, Japan, UK, Mexico, Australia, Hong Kong, and Taiwan. The top cities were New York, Chicago, LA, Atlanta, Miami, Toronto, London, Shanghai, and San Juan. They log in to the Williams Williams & McKissick site or Auction Network® to watch, bid, and win.

Currently, of the more than 10,000 real estate auctions Williams

& Williams® conducted in 2011, 89 percent received a bid through Auction Network®. Twenty-nine percent of the time, the high bidder or winner was someone logged on and bidding remotely through Auction Network®, simultaneously competing with bidders standing on site at the property. Since its inception, Auction Network® has increased the high bids across all our real estate sales by 9 to 11 percent, meaning even if the high bidder is someone standing on the lawn bidding in person, the people bidding remotely on Auction Network® are driving the high bid up as they compete for the home. It's exciting to see someone bidding from England on a property in Greenwich, Connecticut or someone in Dallas bidding on a home in Georgia. To say that we at Williams, Williams & McKissick™ are huge advocates of technology is an understatement.

That said, it will never replace standing in the crowd in front of that property looking those bidders in the eye and watching the excitement build, for the same reason seeing Lady Gaga live on stage is not the same as listening to the CD.

I created and founded Auction Network®, my senior team brought it to life, and my business partner Dean Williams stood behind it financially, spending millions to allow interactive auctions into bedrooms and boardrooms.

Auction Network®'s real-time interactive bidding and auction programming is fabulous. It allows bidders who might not have shown up otherwise—those who simply can't make the trip or prefer the anonymity—to bid from afar. It brings bidders from across the US and around the world, broadening the market from local and state-wide, to a regional and national audience. Someone in Nevada might think the real estate prices in Georgia are wonderful as they compete against a Georgian standing in front of the property who thinks they shouldn't go any higher.

Equally fabulous is the live auction and the skilled auctioneer who addresses a crowd on the lawn in Phoenix, entertaining and capti-vating you and making you understand this is the opportunity of a lifetime. If that auctioneer can look you in the eye, he'll always convince you of something...most likely that you should bid one more time.

Technology's goal should be to deliver auctions to buyers anywhere they are, in any format they desire, on every screen...iPhone®, laptop, TV, computer, wristwatch, and virtual desktop...from bedroom to boardroom to ballroom.

But remember, technology doesn't make a great auction...it's an exciting window *into* a great auction. You still have to choose your auction company for great auctioneering, smart marketing, and proven results. If you've covered the basics, then technology is the bonus.

# Chapter 24

## Personal Property Can Be Very Personal

You've watched *Antiques Roadshow* enough to know that occasionally the guy lugging the atrocious ceramic monkey his mom left him in her will, finds out the china chimp's worth more than his house. You fantasize about a sack of doubloons in an attic trunk or an original copy of the Declaration of Independence rolled up inside the wall of your newly purchased home.

The issue is always provenance. It isn't enough that your Aunt Hattie told you that her great-great-uncle Jeremiah brought this book back from the Civil War and that Ulysses S. Grant personally signed it for him. That kind of story is always interesting to buyers and may make them want the item even more, but to assure that the big money bids, you must have proof of authenticity. The sale of anything exceptionally valuable must be accompanied by provenance, documentation that proves authenticity via chain of ownership. Think of it like the pedigree paperwork for your expensive pup. The pup is no less loveable or valuable to the family without paperwork, but if you intend to sell the pup, you'll get more money if he has papers.

So don't be offended if you can't find the paperwork and therefore the auction company refuses to offer the item as authentic. They can state that they believe it to be an original, but they have no paperwork and it's caveat emptor.

If your auction company stumbles across a Van Gogh in your attic, they should call a firm who specializes in rare art and determine how best to handle that portion of the sale. For the vast majority of personal items that go to auction, your auction company can consult specialists or research the item and arrive at a marketing strategy on their own.

Auction of personal property is labor intensive and usually costs the seller a much larger commission, ranging anywhere from 15-35 percent. Personal-property auctions require organization, speed of presentation, and a good auction team. Success hinges either on great product handled flawlessly or lots of product handled rapidly.

Small mom-and-pop auction houses take items on consignment or go to estates and buy the entire house full of goods for one low price and then resell them at their auction houses. Think about the labor involved. They have to load the entire household like a moving company, take it to their auction barn, unload it, label it, clean it up, and often make sure it's in working order, display it, market it, and sell it every thirty days. If they hold an auction every week, they're making consignment or purchase trips, transporting, cataloguing, marketing, displaying in the same week that they're arranging payment and picking up hundreds of items from the last auction. Small auction houses have told me that on some sale days the concession stand carries the day, making more money than the auction. Personal-property auction houses should be applauded. They're the roots of the industry.

Personal property is often more emotionally laden than real estate. After all, you've bought and sold properties over the years, but you've carried some personal items with you throughout your entire life.

For four decades we had a family cabin in northern Minnesota. All my growing up was tied to that cabin. Barely twenty, I commissioned a craftsman deep in the birch woods to build me a parson's table out of north-woods pine and red and yellow oak. It was a smooth, sleek, eight-foot-long coffee table in the day when coffee tables reigned supreme in living rooms. Over the years, it traveled from Minnesota to Oklahoma, to Los Angeles, Florida, and back. It lived in attics, garages, mini storage, and PODS®. It was always too large to go anywhere and so I stored it again. But I would never give it up. Forty years later, it has just had leg extensions added to it and is a conference table in my office. If I can drag a coffee table that large across the US with me for four decades, you can only imagine that I would carry items from my dear deceased grandmother on my back across the Mojave before I would let them be sold for nothing. Personal property is very...personal.

So I understand, when talking to sellers about their personal property, why it takes ten times longer than discussions surrounding the real estate. In the case of one seller, his artwork meant everything—his entire home had been designed as a palette for the art. The paintings were a reminder of his time spent with a very talented fellow artist now deceased. Do you think the seller wanted money for the paintings? Of course, but not for money's sake. He wanted the price paid for the paintings to demonstrate respect for the artist and for his own good taste in talent and friendship. If the art was sold for next to nothing, then part of the seller's life meant nothing. The seller was selling all the artwork Absolute...except for one painting. He had to be sure that one painting sold for more than all the others. It had to. It was the best, the most important, meant the most to him. And so he separated that painting from the rest and placed a reserve on it. That painting sold for two-and-a-half times the reserve. It was as critical to the sale as his real estate and may have made him happier.

Being specialists in the auction of real estate, we used to think of the personal property as just the "remaining household items."

Today we know that the seller only feels validated, and the auction a success, if those personal items are treated with love and respect, and we have now swung to the opposite end of the pendulum. We try to piece together the story of the items, where they came from and why the seller bought them, and convey that in the personalized Web site we create for his sale. Auction Network® photographs and videotapes each of those items individually, and on auction day they're streamed live for remote viewers and bidders and for the attending audience at the live auction.

Some companies auction nothing but personal property, just as some handle only real estate. It's difficult to have two separate auction companies trying to manage your sale simultaneously. Usually the seller selects the real estate auction company and they either handle everything or bring in personal-property, farm-equipment, or cattle auctioneers. Ask the auction house you're thinking of hiring to show you examples of how they've handled personal-property sales—look at the printed materials, Web site, video—and find out how successful they've been at selling it.

Why do sellers get so hung up on the small things? Because they feel they may not know what the real estate will bring, but they do know the saltshaker is worth fifty dollars because that's what they paid for it. And sometimes, as in my case, it's their "coffee table." It represents all my growing up in the north woods, the first time I made any money and could actually pay someone to custom-build something, and how cool I thought my own design was and how I cherished every compliment about that table over the years. Selling it too low or to someone who was rather indifferent about it would confirm I was crazy for carrying it around with me all those years. And so if it ever went to auction, I would not be happy with a value based on wood and glue. It would have to bring *more* than its worth, because it's priceless to me.

As you think about your own sale, create a list of the items that you really care about—the very special ones—and make the list in this order:

1. I will keep these and always have them with me because they are priceless memories:
   - The jewelry box my great-grandmother gave me.
   - The old hammer and saw my father used when he opened his first hardware store.
2. I will donate these items because they will never bring anything of monetary value but they will be very meaningful to the receiver:
   - Old medical equipment to church groups doing work in foreign countries.

- Old photographs of downtown to the historical society.

3. I will only let these items go to the right kind of person or company:
    - Medical books I would like a young grad student to buy.
    - Antique horse carriage I would like a museum to buy.

4. I will sell these but with a reserve. They must bring the right amount of money or I won't let them go.

5. I will sell these Absolute. Extra money is my end goal.

Use the list to discuss which items the auction company can really help you with and how they intend to market them. Obviously categories one and two are for the seller to handle. Category three should be handled by the seller; however, the auction company can make suggestions or phone calls, and attempt to match the right buyer. Categories four and five are clearly auction-company concerns.

Too often sellers begin with the idea that everything is category five and then throughout the marketing process begin sorting, pulling, and fretting over their belongings. It's much better to be clear in your own mind where these pieces of your life belong before auction marketing begins, then let the auction company assist once you've made the list. Or you can do it like most sellers do:

> *This I cherish*
>
> *This I don't*
>
> *This I'll donate*
>
> *This I won't*
>
> *Just sell this for what it brings*
>
> *Oh hell, just sell the whole damned thing!*

# CHAPTER 25

## BREAKING OUT OF THE BOX

If we could see ourselves clearly from outer space, we would agree that we are, indeed, the box people. Our planet is divided into grids of longitude and latitude. Our real estate is divided by government mandate into a system of six-mile-square boxes called townships. Those squares are further divided into one-mile sections of land containing 640 acres each, and those acres are again divided into squares and rectangles of 160, 80, 40, 20 until we move into the city and divide our land into blocks and lots, onto which we build boxes we call home. Inside the boxes, we sleep in box beds, we shower in stalls, which are boxes with water, we eat a good deal of our food out of boxes, and we drive SUVs that resemble boxes. So is it any wonder that we have trouble mentally getting "out of the box" when it comes to how we think about dispersing our real estate? But staying in your home for months and years past the moment you wish to move transitions you from being Lord of the Manor to King of the Box.

This book has asked you to break out of the box—rethink *everything* you've ever been taught about real estate: the way you value it, list it, and sell it. So let's recap.

1.  Most individual sellers who choose auction are doing it to assist in a life transition: moving to a new job, getting a divorce, downsizing for retirement, or upsizing for an expanding family.

2.  Property sold at auction by a reputable talented auction company always "get what it's worth," which may or may not match the number in your head, but it is current market value. Holding on to the number in your head when you can't get anyone to agree with you, by writing you a check for that amount, will steal days of your life, give you sleepless nights, and cost you a good deal of money in "holding" costs...or the cost of holding on.

3.  Auction never destroys neighborhood values, it re-aligns them. Once an auction is held, real estate agents will tell you that their listed homes start to sell because buyers and sellers alike are now confident about values.

4. Auction puts you in control. You select the day you want to sell, and sell in thirty days.

5. Auction pulls buyers off the sidelines and forces them to compete.

6. Auction is life changing. If you like life the way it is, list and wait. If you want to change your life, call the auction company, and then call the movers.

7. Auction delivers personal freedom. If your home has been holding you hostage, auction will unchain you from your real estate.

8. Middlemen are simply the people you pay to stand between you and what you want.

9. "Laying low" until the market recovers is not a strategy; it's a position.

# CHAPTER 26

## TAKE THE QUIZ:
### IS REAL ESTATE AUCTION RIGHT FOR YOU?

So now you're ready to answer the auction quiz to find out if you're an auction convert.

The information in this book is often shared with potential sellers who contact us. Read the questions below and answer them true or false from your own personal point of view:

**True/False. Then select one option from question ten.**

| | | | |
|---|---|---|---|
| 1. | I have a number in my head and I can't let go of it. | **T** | **F** |
| 2. | I don't need to sell my house, but I am curious what it would bring at auction. | **T** | **F** |
| 3. | I like expert advice and support, versus relying on myself. | **T** | **F** |
| 4. | An auction sign in my front yard would embarrass me. | **T** | **F** |

5.   Some information about my real estate is off limits.            T  F

6.   Current market value is better than setting a list price.        T  F

7.   Auction is a strategy versus a distress signal.                  T  F

8.   I like quick change in my life.                                  T  F

9.   I know how much my real estate is costing me every month.        T  F

10.  The following would get better if I sold my house at auction?

**(Select one from a-j.)**

a.   My finances would improve.

b.   I would have more time to do things I like to do.

c.   I would have fewer responsibilities.

d.   I would be able to relocate to a new property, town, or state.

e.   I could finally move on with my life.

f.   It would put an end to haunting memories.

g.   My family would be happier as a result.

h.   I would be happier as a result.

i.   I might have some extra cash to do other things.

j.   Nothing would really get better if I sold my house.

**Auction Angst:**   If you answered TRUE to questions 1, 2, and chose 10j, regardless of how you answered the other questions, it would be very difficult for you to sell at auction. I would suggest you either don't sell right now or contact a real estate agent and let them work with you.

**Almost Auction:** If you answered FALSE to questions 1,2, 3, 4, 5, and didn't choose 10j, you are halfway there. You simply need to spend some time with a good auction company and talk about selling your property.

**Auction Advocate:** If you answered FALSE to questions 1-5 and TRUE to questions 6,7,8,9 and didn't choose 10j, what are you waiting for? You're an auction advocate!

**If you want to experience selling your home at auction, you can take the next step by going to:**

- www.williamsauction.com and check out all the homes we sell every month across the US.
- www.auctionnetwork.com and Watch Bid and Win.
- Phone (1-800-801-8003) and Sr. VPs Rob Bridges or Fontana Fitzwilson will direct you to the right sales exec.
- Click the "sell my home" button on our Web site and fill out the seller's information form.

Auction your home? Absolutely! Hundreds of thousands of people sold their real estate at auction in 2011, not because they had to but because they chose to. Auction has moved beyond the early adopters and has reached the tipping point, moving into mainstream America. Auction will become the primary way real estate is traded in the future for many smart people, like you, who want to take control of their lives, sell, and move on.

Many of our Williams, Williams & McKissick™ department heads, sales people, marketing people, senior staff, and board members have sold their homes at auction through our company, and of course I have as well, and wouldn't sell any other way.

Giving up the old way of selling for auction is like giving up ox carts for UPS, phone booths for cell phones, rabbit ears for wireless, list-and-wait for sell-it-in-thirty-days. Once you experience the speed and convenience and efficiency of auction, you'll never go back. See you at the next Williams & Williams™ auction!

# About the Author

Pamela L. McKissick is co-owner and Chief Executive Officer of Williams, Williams & McKissick (WWM), LLC, the parent company to Williams & Williams® Worldwide Real Estate Auction, Auction Network®, and WWM Exchange™. Pam oversees all aspects of the WWM businesses and drives the strategic vision for the company, including a live on-site, online, onscreen platform that re-invents the way real estate is bought and sold. Building on Williams & Williams' rich auction history, Pam is leading the company's mission to empower the open exchange of real estate worldwide.

Pam has a successful track record for building organizations into major brands. She joined Williams & Williams in 2005 as Chief Operating Officer and built a sustainable business model that afforded the company year-over-year expansion and diversification, selling over 50,000 assets valued at more than $5 billion. In 2007, Pam founded Auction Network (www.auctionnetwork.com), a 24-hour streaming television network that allows viewers to participate remotely in live auctions taking place throughout the world and bid interactively, in real time. Auction Network presents over a thousand live real estate auctions every month, overcoming consumers' fears regarding the purchase of high-value real estate assets instantaneously with the click of a button.

In 2010, Pam entered into an equal partnership with Dean Williams, former sole shareholder of Williams & Williams, and formed WWM, creating one of the largest, most cutting-edge and diverse auction firms in the world.

Prior to joining Williams & Williams, Pam enjoyed an extensive career in television and entertainment. She was president and COO of TV Guide Television Group, co-owner of McKissick Gregory Productions in Hollywood, held key leadership positions for Walt Disney World, and was VP Network Specials for Disney Studios. Among her notable accomplishments, Pam spearheaded the launch of Walt Disney World's Epcot Center and was the first woman broadcaster for WNEW in New York City at the age of eighteen. An established writer, Pam has penned several byline articles on the value of real estate and the meaning of auction, which have been printed in notable trade publications such as *DSNews, HousingWire, Mortgage Servicing News,* and *Texas Real Estate Business.*

Pam is a cum laude graduate of Jacksonville University, a graduate of the American Academy of Dramatic Arts in New York, and a trained auctioneer, having earned her degree at World Wide College of Auctioneering and her CAI designation. She is also a licensed real estate agent and is an active member and supporter of the National Auctioneers Association.

Made in the USA
San Bernardino, CA
10 May 2016